Polynesian
Navigation
AND THE
DISCOVERY OF
New Zealand

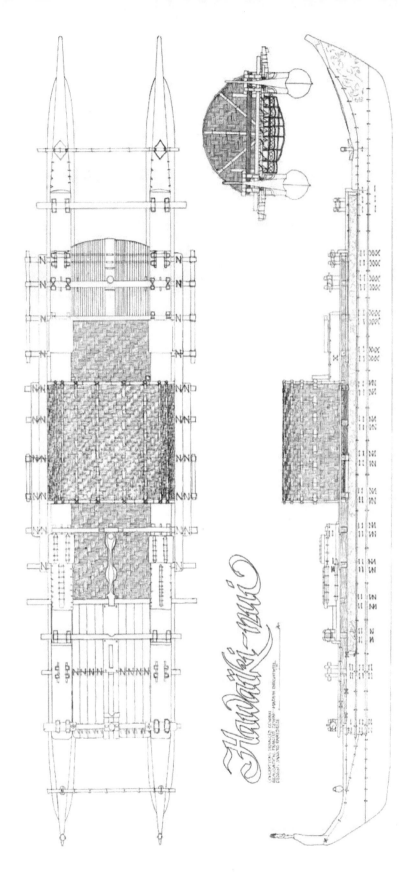

Scale drawing of the traditional voyaging canoe, Hawaiki-nui

Polynesian Navigation AND THE DISCOVERY OF New Zealand

JEFF EVANS

Foreword by Francis Cowan

Oratia

In loving memory of my mother,
Shirlee Francis Evans
(31 May 1934–22 November 1997)

Published by Oratia Books, Oratia Media Ltd, 783 West Coast Road, Oratia,
Auckland 0604, New Zealand (www.oratia.co.nz).

ISBN 978-0-947506-40-7

First published 1998 as The Discovery of Aotearoa by Reed Books (NZ)
Second edition 2011 by Libro International
Reprinted 2014
This edition 2017 by Oratia Books

Illustrations: Philip Lockhart, Jonette Surridge
Photographs: Geoff Moon (31), Bob Maysmor/Porirua Museum (36), Jeff Evans
(19, 79, 123), Alessandra Zecchini (44), Herman Helmuth (83, 96, 101, 103),
Alice Cowan (114), Matahi Brightwell (all other photos)
Cover: Kennett Watkins, Departure of the Six Canoes from Rarotonga to
New Zealand, 1906, Auckland Art Gallery/Toi o Tamaki

Printed in New Zealand

CONTENTS

Part Two: In the wake of Kupe 75

List of Maps

FOREWORD

I would like to shed some light on traditional Polynesian navigation. Ancient navigation was but dead reckoning, without compass, and integrating the observation of the stars. The sky, when clear, can give a lot of information on numerous destinations — but even then, one must have a lot of experience.

The technique of this ancient art was based on a very good knowledge of the movements of the stars and, of course, geography. It is against logic to say geography doesn't come into navigation in today's age, because all the islands of our world are known. There can no longer be 'voyages of discovery'. Today no navigator can escape the fact that he knows where he is sailing to. In fact, before starting on a journey, a navigator must know about his destination and prepare his route according to that knowledge. But there is still an incredible amount of skill involved — no less than when our ancestors were sailing hundreds of years ago. Navigators must still have a very good knowledge of the heavens and the sea.

When passing on knowledge about how to navigate from one destination to another, the ancient people taught partly through oral traditions, but mainly through practice. This was necessary because when the sky is covered over with cloud, one has to find clues in the movements of the wind and sea when deciding on the course to sail. This is often too hard to explain verbally.

For those who might be interested, the practice of navigation without instruments is still taught at various islands throughout the Pacific in traditional settings, as well as in the more modern setting of Honolulu, and it is a good thing.

In 1983, I joined in partnership with my son-in-law Matahi Brightwell and the partial sponsorship of OTAC (Tahiti Cultural Centre) to complete the construction of a 22-m double canoe which Matahi had started in New Zealand. The canoe, Hawaiki-nui, was constructed using logs hollowed out with axes and adzes and entirely held together by sennit ropes (woven coconut fibres) and wooden dowels. The hulls were assembled together in the ancient traditional way, and the rigging was held together by manila ropes. No metal fastenings were used, and at that particular time, one could say that it was the only double canoe built by traditional techniques and materials.

Hawaiki-nui was launched in 1984, and in late 1985, after twelve months of trials and refinements, we departed on a voyage from Tahiti to Aotearoa, via Ra'iatea and Rarotonga. We were to follow the course believed to have been used hundreds of years ago by the ancestors of the Maori during their migration voyages to Aotearoa. That we were able to complete the voyage unaided and relying entirely on Polynesian navigation techniques perhaps goes some way to proving the sailing ability of our ancestors, as well as the durability of their waka.

Our voyage created a lot of interest throughout the Pacific, and a number of projects sprung up building canoes for offshore sailing. This concerted effort was very positive, and it is hoped that other Polynesian islands will also try to follow that path. My only regret is that none of these canoes followed the same traditional construction that was used in Hawaiki-nui.

Francis Cowan, 1998

Francis Cowan is recognised as one of the greatest Polynesian navigators and canoe builders of modern times. He took part in the Tahiti-nui expedition from Tahiti to Chile in the 1950s, and led the Hawaiki-nui expedition that is described in part two of this book.

ACKNOWLEDGEMENTS

Firstly I would like to thank Matahi and Raipoia Brightwell for their open and unreserved hospitality during the several trips I made to their Gisborne home. The warmth you both extended to me made these visits a pleasure.

To Francis Cowan, thank you for your input and your patience, and especially for the opportunity to share in your reminiscences. It was an honour I won't forget.

The support and guidance of Peter Janssen and Peter Dowling of Reed Publishing certainly helped keep things running smoothly (and almost to schedule!). Thank you both.

Finally, I couldn't have hoped to complete this book without the support of my wife. Fuli, thank you for always being there.

INTRODUCTION

The discovery of Aotearoa by Polynesian navigators is acknowledged as one of the last great geographical discoveries in the Pacific, if not the world. Sailing into uncharted waters, faced with the possibility of encountering currents and winds that would leave them beyond hope of returning to their homeland, these men possessed the courage to sail for as long as five or six weeks to an unknown destination. Fortunately, they not only discovered a fabulous land, but were able to return to extol the virtues of that land to their kin.

What they found when they finally arrived on the shores of Aotearoa was a land rich in natural resources. Fish and bird life, including the huge moa, was in abundance, and the soil under foot could sustain the root crops that formed such an important part of their daily food intake. Other assets in this wonderful new land included the huge kauri and totara trees that provided incredible amounts of timber for everything from shelter to weapons to canoes, and stone and pounamu (greenstone) suitable for working into the tools needed to shape and form the timber.

Perhaps the most important fact was that this uninhabited island group had room for thousands of people — enough room, in fact, for anyone who wanted to leave the homeland and start a new life. Thus, one of the world's great migrations was about to commence.

This book explores several aspects of the Polynesian discovery of Aotearoa, including aspects of Maori origin, traditional navigation, and the knowledge that has been kept alive over the centuries in karakia, waiata and tradition. It is hoped that it will help the reader to understand this fascinating part of Maori pre-history and to appreciate the incredible skills and courage that belonged to the ancestors of the Maori people.

Starting with an introduction to the peopling of the Pacific, the first chapter looks at the initial thrust into the Pacific from the west along with the subsequent discoveries of Hawaii and Rapa-nui, before suggesting possible determining factors for the exploration down into the cold southern ocean that led to the discovery of Aotearoa.

In the second chapter the homeland of the Maori is discussed, along with many of the theories that have been put forward over the years in an effort to determine its position. Attention is given to the question of whether there was more than one migration, and the possible date or dates for them.

The third chapter offers two versions of the tradition of Kupe's discovery of Aotearoa, and a comprehensive list of places visited by him and his crew during their exploration of Aotearoa.

Navigational lore that survives in Maori waiata, karakia and traditions is brought together in the next chapter, along with contemporary knowledge collected from the likes of David Lewis, Nainoa Thompson of Hokule'a, and Matahi Brightwell and Francis Cowan of Hawaiki-nui.

The fifth chapter gives a contemporary view of traditional Polynesian navigational knowledge, explaining some of the techniques believed to have been employed by navigators during the ancient voyages to Aotearoa and suggesting how they may have learned this exacting skill.

Finally, part two gives us a first-hand account of the building and sailing of the voyaging canoe Hawaiki-nui, which sailed from Tahiti to Aotearoa in late 1985. An incredible voyage, and a remarkable story.

Jeff Evans

A number of readers may be disappointed to discover that an account of the canoe Te Aurere is not included in this book. Preliminary discussions were held with Hekenukumai (Hec) Busby regarding the inclusion of Te Aurere in this work, in order to give a complete account of contemporary Maori voyaging canoes. However, it was agreed not to include Te Aurere's voyages so as not to pre-empt a full account planned for a publication that is currently being worked on.

PART ONE

THE NAVIGATORS OF POLYNESIA

THE PEOPLING OF THE PACIFIC

The ancient Polynesian explorers

The discovery of Aotearoa by Polynesian explorers sometime between AD 500 and 1000[1] was perhaps the last great island discovery by an extraordinary people. At a time when most European seamen were still hugging the shoreline as they sailed from port to port along their coastlines, the Polynesians had already sailed halfway across the vast Pacific Ocean on voyages of discovery.

Originating from the Asian mainland several thousand years ago, the ancestors of the modern-day Polynesians began their expansion into the Pacific by exploring eastwards through the nearby island chains of Indonesia, the Philippines and their close neighbours. Soon after, the islands that comprise the Micronesian, Melanesian and Polynesian groups were also within reach of their voyaging canoes and navigational ability. By the time the Polynesians had settled the island groups stretching from Fiji in the west to the Marquesas in the east, they had proven themselves to be unrivalled as the greatest sailors and explorers of their time.

After a period of consolidation, the next great push by the Polynesian navigators came with the exploration of the Pacific Ocean to the north and south. In the years between the birth of Christ and AD 1000, they discovered the Hawaiian Islands to the north, Rapa-nui (Easter Island) to the south-east, and Aotearoa (New Zealand) to the south-west. Thus, the three points of the so-called Polynesian Triangle were joined. Using skills developed over many generations, Polynesians discovered virtually every island and atoll in the latitudes between Aotearoa and Hawaii, colonising as they went virtually every habitable island and atoll.

Learning to co-exist with their environment was the Polynesians' secret to success, and possibly their greatest achievement. It was not unusual for crews to wait weeks or even months for the right conditions before they would embark on a voyage. Once out at sea, they were in a class of their

1. Dates used are the most accurate estimates available at the time of writing.

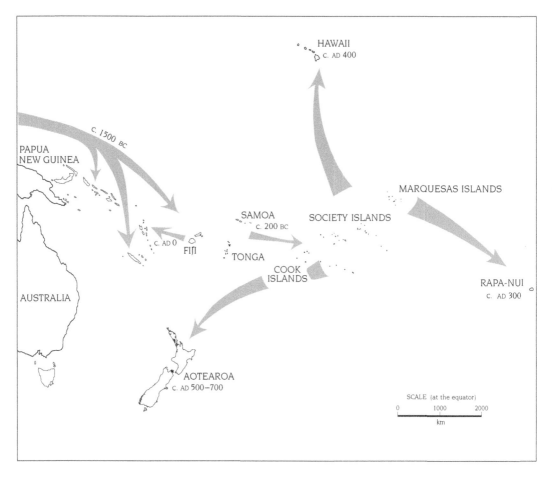

The major migrations in the Pacific, with dates of dispersal.

own. An experienced navigator was able to read the moods and signs of the sea and sky through patience and constant vigilance. They looked at the ocean surface as we might look at a road map. Signs were there for anyone sufficiently trained to see. They understood, for example, that changes to the regular roll of the swell in open ocean meant that the swell had been disrupted by the presence of land, perhaps as much as 160 km distant. Likewise, immobile clouds on the horizon might suggest the presence of land, as it was common for cloud to appear stationary above islands.

Although the skills of Polynesian navigators are deservedly recognised and applauded now, that wasn't the case when European explorers first entered the Pacific. Largely due to preconceived prejudices about the intelligence of a so-called 'savage' and 'uncultured' people, as well as the almost insurmountable problems of inter-cultural communication, Western minds failed to grasp the abilities of Polynesian navigators and the seaworthiness of their vessels.

It was not until Captain James Cook was able to converse with the Tahitian Tupaia that any real appreciation of the Polynesians' skills was acknowledged. With the help of Tupaia, Cook sketched a map of the Tahitian world that stretched from Samoa in the west to the Marquesas in the east, an area not much smaller than the continent of the United States of America.

Despite this and other revelations, historians still publicly doubted the Polynesians' nautical skill well into the second half of the twentieth century. Popular theories throughout most of the nineteenth and twentieth centuries suggested that the Pacific islands were inhabited only by chance, with fishermen and coastal voyagers being swept by unexpected storms to uninhabited lands. As late as the mid-1960s, the historian Andrew Sharp[2] was claiming that the number of fishermen and inter-island travellers that have been reported as lost at sea over the years proved that the Polynesian was no great navigator. However, what Sharp did not appear to take into account was that few fishermen would have been trained navigators, as would few captains of inter-island voyages. The skills required of a captain during a 50-km trip to a neighbouring island, for example, hardly compare to those needed for a three-week voyage of exploration into unfamiliar waters. It is probable that the vast majority of canoes lost at sea would have been captained by coastal fishermen, or at least men with minimal long-distance navigational experience.

Among the many other arguments put forward against the likelihood of the Polynesians having systematically explored and discovered large numbers of Pacific islands, the following two stand out. Firstly, early Europeans in the Pacific didn't consider the Polynesian waka anywhere near strong enough to be used for voyages of any significant distance. Sailing in large wooden vessels held together by nails, the Europeans could not imagine how vessels held together by nothing more than plant fibre and resembling small coastal fishing boats could survive on the open ocean.

Secondly, it was assumed for years by armchair theorists that the trade winds blew non-stop from the east during the voyaging season, thus against the generally accepted direction of discovery. As a result, it was argued that fishermen and the like were probably blown uncontrollably eastward by the winds during the rough, stormy, non-voyaging season, while all of the valuable voyaging waka were safely beached. It wasn't until it was pointed out that there are regular periods of intermittent westerly winds during the trade wind season, lasting upwards of two to three weeks at a time, that this argument was laid to rest.

Indeed, in recent years, computer simulation studies have shown that it is highly unlikely that drift voyages contributed to any great extent to the discovery or habitation of Polynesian islands.[3] Conclusions from the studies,

---

2. Andrew Sharp's book *Ancient Voyagers in the Pacific*, later revised and published as *Ancient Voyagers in Polynesia*, was responsible for much of the renewed interest in Polynesian voyaging in the 1950s and 1960s.
3. For further reading, see Geoff Irwin, *The Prehistoric Exploration and Colonization of the Pacific*.

along with evidence collected from contemporary canoe voyages throughout the Pacific, strongly suggest that deliberate two-way voyaging would have been a critical requirement for the discovery and successful settlement of most, if not all, islands in Polynesia. It was during the breaks in the westerly winds that voyaging waka struck out across the Pacific to the east, keen to take advantage of the following wind, confident in the knowledge that the winds would eventually reverse direction and speed them home.

The discovery of Aotearoa

It is probable that Aotearoa was discovered by 'professional sailors': men dedicated to a life at sea, exploring the oceans for their sponsoring chief. The hunger of chiefs keen to expand their personal domain and power, and the sailors' desire to increase their personal mana or prestige, would be a powerful mix that must surely have inspired many voyages.

While the construction and maintenance of a voyaging waka would have been a considerable burden on any community, there would have been little or no trouble recruiting a crew from within the ranks of an island population. For men who loved to be at sea, whether fishing or voyaging along the well-travelled ara moana (ocean paths) between known islands, the chance to voyage on the open sea would have been hard to resist.

Reasons for voyaging were many. It is often suggested that a major motivation was the desire of younger sons of chiefly families to seek new lands to rule over for themselves, rather than live in the shadow of the eldest son. With land and power usually being passed from father to first-born son, the future prospects for an ambitious younger sibling often lay beyond the horizon. Migration might also have been a necessity after cyclones or tidal waves had devastated smaller low-lying islands and atolls. With coconut trees stripped of their fruit, taro plantations contaminated by flooding sea water, and other sources of food undoubtedly also affected, the inhabitants may have had little or no choice but to seek new lands on which to start over.

A further motive recorded in tradition is that of a pair of lovers fleeing their homeland, and the revenge of the woman's husband. This appears a number of times in Maori tradition, two examples being the stories of Kupe and the waka Matahourua, and Tamatekapua and the waka Te Arawa.

While it is generally accepted by most authorities that Kupe[4] was the traditional discoverer of Aotearoa, there were a number of other early voyagers to the 'Land of the Long White Cloud' whose places in history are not as clear. However, claims that one or more of the following waka reached Aotearoa before Kupe cannot be completely discounted.

4. See the third chapter, 'Kupe's voyage to Aotearoa'.

The navigators reaching Aotearoa encountered an untamed land abounding in natural riches.

Pauiraraira is claimed by some to have been the first waka to voyage to Aotearoa, with Raka-taura as captain. According to tradition, Raka-taura sailed along the coast of the North Island without seeing any sign of habitation. Convinced that he had found an uninhabited island, he returned to Hawaiki, where he passed on the sailing directions to Kupe.

Nukutawhiti is remembered as the waka in which Tuputupu-whenua and Kui voyaged to Aotearoa during the earliest period of discovery. These two figures are often associated with Maui, and are sometimes named as the guardians that Maui left behind to look after the land when he finally returned to Hawaiki.

Huruhurumanu is an ancient waka closely associated with Maori of the South Island Waitaha people. It is said that during the journey to Aotearoa, the waka encountered 50 gigantic seas that threatened to swamp it. The crew were later able to smooth the way, presumably by karakia (prayer or incantation), so that in the years that followed the Uruao and other waka were able to voyage safely in her wake.

Tuahiwi-o-Atea was the waka of Hui-te-Rangiora. It has probably the weakest connection with Aotearoa of the four waka. Polynesian legend claims that on one voyage of exploration, presumably deep into the southern ocean, Hui-te-Rangiora experienced huge seas and encountered seals, bull-kelp and a 'sea of arrowroot' that later historians have suggested might have been an ice-floe.

With Aotearoa having been discovered by navigators sufficiently skilled to return to their homelands after weeks of travel on the open ocean, it can only have been a matter of time before precise voyaging instructions became available and migration voyages commenced. Aotearoa was soon to experience its first permanent human inhabitants.

It is probable that the initial settlements would have been on the warmer east coast of the upper North Island, where imported crops such as kumara, taro and yam would have had a chance to flourish. The first inhabitants would probably have been quick to supplement their food stocks with the abundant fish and birdlife which, as at home, teemed within easy reach of their villages. Even so, they had to adapt to an environment substantially different from the tropical islands they had left. While some of the crops took root and were successfully grown, others, such as coconut trees, failed to survive in the much cooler climate.

Many other problems had to be addressed. For example, the open-sided houses so widely seen in tropical Polynesia were totally unsuitable in the southern winters and needed to be redesigned, as did clothes. Likewise, some of the hooks and lures used for catching specific varieties of fish were either entirely useless or less effective here and had to be redesigned.

Other challenges surfaced later, when new arrivals were forced to spread progressively throughout the North and South Islands as the more favoured regions became fully inhabited. In the South Island, the harsh climate prevented many crops from growing, and new food sources were needed to feed the increasing population. The huge flightless moa, thought to have been hunted to extinction, was one casualty of this enforced change of diet. Sea lion and seal numbers were also put under increased pressure by the need to supplement the meagre crops that survived. Adaptation to Aotearoa's sometimes harsh environment, and a full understanding of the ecological balance on both land and sea, would have been an ongoing process that probably took a number of generations to achieve.

THE HOMELAND OF THE MAORI

Hawaiki-nui, Hawaiki-roa, Hawaiki-pamamao —
the ancestral homeland of the Maori.

Early theories

The search for the origins of the first Maori has often been a misguided affair. By the time Europeans started to take a real interest in the subject at the end of the nineteenth century and the beginning of the twentieth, much of the knowledge orally passed down over the centuries from one generation to the next had been lost. With the onset of large-scale European colonisation in the mid-1800s, many Maori were quick to embrace the European world, and discarded their traditional schools and ways of learning.

Despite this loss of knowledge, or perhaps because of it, theories have abounded on the question of Maori origins. Cook and his fellow explorers, who visited these shores in 1769 on board the *Endeavour*, were among the first to note the similarity between the customs and language of the Maori and those of other Polynesians. The ease with which Cook's Tahitian companion Tupaia managed to converse with a number of coastal tribes is obvious when reading through the various journals kept by Cook and his crew. The sole American on board the *Endeavour*, James Magra, wrote the following telling observation in his journal.[1]

> It deserves to be remarked, that the people of New Zealand spoke the language of Otahitee with but very little difference, not so much as is found between many counties in England; a circumstance of the most extraordinary kind, and must necessarily lead us conclude, that one of these places originally peopled from the other, though they are near two thousand miles distance; and nothing but the ocean intervenes, which we should hardly believe they could navigate so far in canoes, the only vessels that they appear to have ever possessed.

1. J.C. Beaglehole, ed., *The Journals of Captain James Cook on his Voyages of Discovery*: 243.

Sir Joseph Banks also accompanied Cook during this first voyage to the Pacific. In his position as botanist and natural historian, Banks closely observed and compared the many island cultures the ship visited throughout Polynesia. While in New Zealand, he compiled a comparative list of words from the Northern Maori, Southern Maori and Tahitian languages. The project was completed with the help of Sydney Parkinson, who collected the southern vocabulary; and possibly Tupaia, who probably assisted with the Tahitian list, although Banks had a fairly good grasp of Tahitian himself. The closeness of the languages is illustrated on the facing page in the comparative list compiled by Banks.[2]

By the end of the nineteenth century a large number of enthusiastic amateur historians were beginning to put forward theories on the homeland of the Maori. Unfortunately their combined efforts managed to retard rather than advance the search. Theories based on exaggerated genealogies and traditions that had been strung together from a number of dubious sources and influenced by biblical stories were the fashion of the day, and held sway over the public for many years.

Included among these theories was that of the Anglican missionary Richard Taylor, who claimed that the Maori were one of the lost tribes of Israel. Taylor went on to suggest that on each successive move away from the root of Western civilisation, as they moved across continents and from island to island, the Maori degenerated into 'the lowest stage of degradation', that is, the 'savages' he saw before him.

Others looked towards the human sciences for the answer. Some studied material culture, while Ernst Dieffenbach and companions looked towards phrenology (the study of the conformation of the skull as an indication of mental faculties), and A.S. Thompson applied craniometry (the science of measuring the skull). Edward Tregear rather imaginatively managed to find in the Maori language a direct link to the Aryan peoples of India and the Iranian plateau.

In an effort to save what little indigenous knowledge remained at the turn of the century, S. Percy Smith, John White, Elsdon Best and others started to collect traditions from wherever possible. Unfortunately, much of the information collected is now considered questionable, especially in the case of John White and S. Percy Smith, as they accepted the information provided by their Maori informants without question. Also, the method used in collecting traditions for White's six-volume work, *The Ancient History of the Maori*, seems unreliable and unprofessional by today's standards. White sent notebooks to several tribal areas and asked that sacred traditions be entrusted to him with pen and paper. Not only did he not have the opportunity to personally question those who were doing the recording for him, but he couldn't even be entirely sure that those elders who had the knowledge were being interviewed.

2. From John Hawkesworth, *An Account of the Voyages Undertaken by the Order of His Majesty for Making Discoveries in the Southern Hemisphere*, vol. 3: 408–409.

English	Northern Maori	Southern Maori	Tahitian
a chief	eareete	eareete	earee
a man	taat	taata	taata
a woman	wahine	wahine	wahine
the head	eupo	heaowpoho	eupo
the hair	macauwe	heoooo	roourou
the ear	terringa	hetaheyei	terrea
the forehead	erai	heai	erai
the eyes	mata	hemata	mata
the cheeks	paparinga	hepapaeh	paparea
the nose	ahewh	heeih	ahew
the mouth	hangoutou	hegowai	outou
the chin	ecouwai	hekaoewi	-
the arm	haringaringa	-	rima
the finger	maticara	hemaigawh	maneow
the belly	ateraboo	-	oboo
the navel	apeto	hecapeeto	peto
come here	haromai	horomai	harromai
fish	heica	heica	eyca
a lobster	kooura	kooure	oure
coccos	taro	taro	taro
sweet potatoes	cumala	cumala	cumala
yams	tuphwhe	tuphwhe	tuphwhe
birds	maanu	maanu	maanu
no	kaoure	kaoure	oure
one	tahai	-	tahai
two	rua	-	rua
three	torou	-	torou
four	ha	-	hea
five	rema	-	rema
six	ono	-	ono
seven	etu	-	hetu
eight	warou	-	warou
nine	iva	-	heva
ten	angahourou	-	ahourou
the teeth	heenihu	heneaho	nihio
the wind	mehow	-	mattai
a thief	amootoo	-	teto
to examine	mataketake	-	mataitai
to sing	eheara	-	heiva
bad	keno	keno	eno
trees	eratou	eratou	eraou
grandfather	toubouna	toubouna	toubouna

Joseph Banks' comparative list of Polynesian languages

Of further concern was the fact that he was limited to employing informants who were literate, and that he paid for the information being collected. How much of White's work is genuine tradition, and how much is fiction, added to fill pages and pockets, will never be known. Soon after the publication of his volumes, however, there was a loud outcry from Maori in many parts of the country claiming that the text contained many errors, and that in many cases large sections of tradition were missing altogether.

Similarly, the work of Smith has been criticised in later years. Relying heavily on manuscripts dictated by Te Matorohanga and a number of his contemporaries from the Wairarapa region in the 1860s, Smith erred in his wholesale acceptance of their contents.

Common in Te Matorohanga's dictations were details seemingly too specific to have been authentic. An example, highlighted by Te Rangi Hiroa (Peter Buck) in his *The Coming of the Maori*, was the description of the original tangata whenua.[3]

> *The people were tall and upright (kokau), with large bones (nunui nga iwi), prominent knees (turi takoto), flat faces (kanohi paraha), quick eyes (mata kanae) that were side glancing (tiro pikari), flat noses (ihu patiki), expanded nostrils (pongare kau parari), straight hair (makawe torotika), some with lank hair (he mahora etahi) and reddish-black skins (kiri puwhero waitutu). They were a people who hugged the fire (he iwi kiri ahi) and they were lazy (mangere). In a later reference it is stated that they had thin calves (ateate rere).*

Buck gives the following comment.

> *The above description would have done credit to a trained physical anthropologist and it would have been remarkable as an example of transmission by memorising over a number of centuries, if it were true. Such characteristics as flat noses with expanded nostrils, thin calves, and reddish-black skins led Percy Smith and Elsdon Best to accept the recital as confirming a theory that the first settlers were of Melanesian stock. However, the details, impressive though they seem, contain one item which destroys their value as an accurate description of racial stock. A constant character of the Melanesian people is their woolly hair and as the hair of the early settlers is definitely stated to be straight (torotika) and lank (mahora), their Melanesian origin cannot be accepted as being supported by the Matorohanga account. It is evident that the Matorohanga school believed that the early settlers were different from themselves and so they made them different. The sum of physical differences formed an academic type that did not exist in real life.*

3. Te Rangi Hiroa, *The Coming of the Maori*: 10–11.

Contemporary theories

In contrast to these early theorists, who had limited resources, contemporary scholars are able to take a much more scientific approach to the problem. Prehistorians today are able to utilise the resources of a number of academic disciplines in order to test their theories, including ethnology, ecology, linguistics, archaeology, and biological anthropology (which takes in DNA testing).

Linguists tell us that the various dialects of Maori fit best into the Eastern Polynesian subgroup of Polynesian languages. The languages most closely related to Maori include those from the Cook Islands, the Society Islands, the Marquesas, Easter Island and Hawaii. In linguistic terms, these languages are grouped together under the title Proto Central-Eastern Polynesian. More specifically, recent research suggests that the dialects from the East Coast of the North Island have especially close links with the languages of the southern Cooks. South Island speech also has a strong southern Cook Island influence, but also seems to have a distinct Marquesan strain entwined in it.

Archaeologists, on the other hand, consider the comparison of artefacts to be a more reliable guide for linking ancient civilisations, although they acknowledge that precise conclusions are difficult. For example, at present there is a significant shortage of suitable artefacts from the Eastern Polynesian islands confirmed as having been manufactured at the approximate time of the Maori migration to Aotearoa. For any reliable conclusion to be drawn, it would be preferable for a whole range of artefacts to be found in the two areas under investigation, with several pairings showing the same distinctive features.

Despite this, archaeologists are confident that the Maori came from Eastern Polynesia, the Society–Marquesan area in particular. Comparisons between artefacts found in ancient burial grounds in Aotearoa and both the Society Islands and the Marquesas show distinctive parallels that leave little doubt in the minds of many archaeologists of the closeness of the cultures. Artefacts documented from the various burial sites include personal ornaments, fish-hooks and stone adzes.

However, a major difficulty facing linguists and archaeologists in the task of settling on a homeland for the Maori is that there have been so many changes in the language and material culture of both Aotearoa and Eastern Polynesia over the centuries. That process of change was accelerated markedly by European colonisation and subsequent economic development. Many archaeological sites have been found throughout Aotearoa, but the majority of these would probably have been left by communities that had been long established in their particular area, making it virtually pointless to compare artefacts. How long it would take a group of new settlers to grow large enough in number to leave this kind of evidence is debatable.

A small founding population situated in a large coastal area, for example, might conceivably take many generations to build up to a size large enough to leave their mark on the land. This is especially true if they moved with the seasons, for example, from seashore, to forest, to lake. The vast majority of the first settlers' personal effects are unlikely ever to be found, leaving us to study the few artefacts from Eastern Polynesia that have been uncovered in New Zealand, along with a larger number that were created in Aotearoa within two or three centuries of the initial migration.

Another problem has been that evidence from unrelated sciences has sometimes been in conflict. While most clues point to the Marquesan–Society region, some bone studies suggest that the closest relatives to the Maori come from the Western Polynesian islands of Samoa and Tonga.

Despite these irregularities and the numerous other challenges that face researchers today, a consensus of sorts has been reached by most contemporary prehistorians. From the evidence currently available, the most likely homeland of the Maori is agreed to lie within the Eastern Polynesian region. Included in the primary group of islands under consideration are the Society Islands (encompassing Tahiti, Ra'iatea and Borabora, among others) and the islands of the Marquesan archipelago. Secondary possibilities include the Southern Cooks, Mangareva, Pitcairn and islands of the Austral archipelago and the Tuamotuan archipelago.

A further point to consider is whether there was a single migration to Aotearoa, other migrations subsequent to the first wave from the same island, or several expeditions from separate islands over an extended period. Unfortunately, the answer to these questions is also hampered by a lack of physical evidence.

Current linguistic evidence, as noted above, points towards more than one Eastern Polynesian island group being represented in Aotearoa, as evidenced by a Marquesan strain found in the southern Cook Island language that has eventually evolved into the current South Island Maori dialect. Furthermore, it is considered highly probable that the convergence of the two languages occurred in Aotearoa after settlement, rather than in Central or Eastern Polynesia during the migratory process. However, until evidence from other disciplines, such as items of material culture (for example hooks, adzes, or personal items of adornment) can back up the linguistic theories, it is not possible to provide a definite answer.

When did they arrive?

Finally, we come to the question of when the Maori discovered Aotearoa. Early theorists, in particular S. Percy Smith, concentrated on genealogical tables collected from Maori at or shortly before the turn of the nineteenth century. They commonly allocated 25 years per generation, and working back from those genealogies they had managed to collect, settled on AD 1350 as the date of the arrival of the migration waka.[4] They did note, however, that other explorers to Aotearoa, such as the well-known Kupe, may have come several hundred years earlier.

Current opinion among scientists offers a wide selection of dates to choose from. The vast majority opt for a date somewhere between AD 700 and AD 1000, although with the qualifier 'on the basis of current evidence'. Most of the remainder argue for dates within two to three hundred years either side of this range.

Unfortunately, despite the ongoing efforts of numerous academics and other researchers, the problem is a lack of substantiated scientific evidence to support any of these claims. Doug Sutton comments in his book, *The Origins of the First New Zealanders*, that 'Only a very limited amount of archaeological research has been done to date on the early period in Northland, the Bay of Plenty and areas of the East Coast.' When one looks at the map of documented landing sites of voyaging waka (see pages 28–29), it will be seen that approximately two-thirds of the recorded landing sites in Aotearoa were between Northland and the East Coast. As it would be reasonable to assume that a fair number of the initial settlements would be located in the general vicinity of the landing sites, a concerted effort is now needed to uncover archaeological sites along the East Coast of the North Island, from the Poverty Bay region northwards. This would allow detailed evaluations to be made by archaeologists using modern methods and equipment. Until we have an abundance of evidence, supported across several disciplines, we will be left with no alternative other than to advance qualified theories.

4. The general acceptance of this date, along with the available genealogical tables which featured a small number of ancestral waka, led to S. Percy Smith's erroneous claim that there was a great migration to Aotearoa by the ancestors of the Maori in AD 1350. First published in 1898, this theory was quoted so often in official histories and educational publications that it became accepted for most of the following 80 years. It was finally successfully refuted by David Simmons in his book *The Great New Zealand Myth* in 1976, although Smith's version is still widely accepted by the general public.

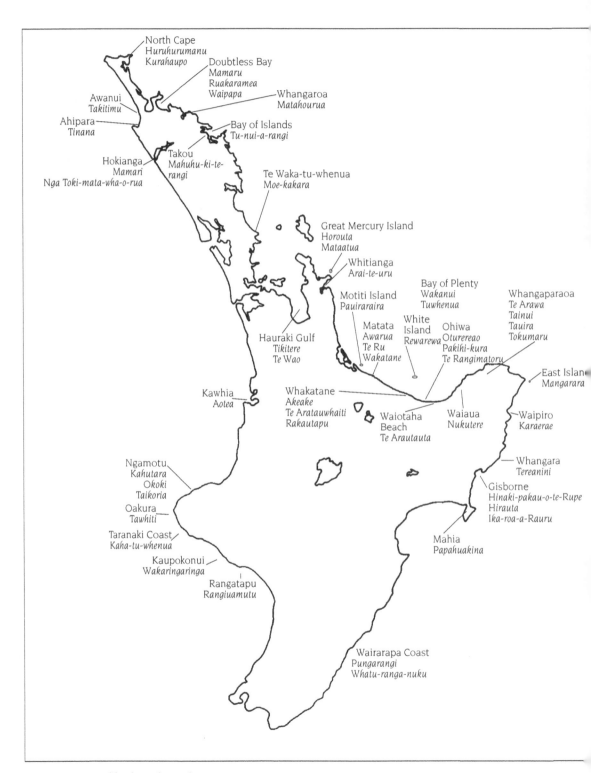

North Cape
Huruhurumanu
Kurahaupo

Doubtless Bay
Mamaru
Ruakaramea
Waipapa

Whangaroa
Matahourua

Awanui
Takitimu

Ahipara
Tinana

Bay of Islands
Tu-nui-a-rangi

Takou
Mahuhu-ki-te-rangi

Hokianga
Mamari
Nga Toki-mata-wha-o-rua

Te Waka-tu-whenua
Moe-kakara

Great Mercury Island
Horouta
Mataatua

Whitianga
Arai-te-uru

Motiti Island
Pauiraraira

Bay of Plenty
Wakanui
Tuwhenua

Whangaparaoa
Te Arawa
Tainui
Tauira
Tokumaru

Matata
Awarua
Te Ru
Wakatane

White Island
Rewarewa

Ohiwa
Oturereao
Pakihi-kura
Te Rangimatoru

East Island
Mangarara

Hauraki Gulf
Tikitere
Te Wao

Kawhia
Aotea

Whakatane
Akeake
Te Aratauwhaiti
Rakautapu

Waiotaha Beach
Te Arautauta

Waiaua
Nukutere

Waipiro
Karaerae

Whangara
Tereanini

Ngamotu
Kahutara
Okoki
Taikoria

Gisborne
Hinaki-pakau-o-te-Rupe
Hirauta
Ika-roa-a-Rauru

Oakura
Tawhiti

Taranaki Coast
Kaha-tu-whenua

Mahia
Papahuakina

Kaupokonui
Wakaringaringa

Rangatapu
Rangiuamutu

Wairarapa Coast
Pungarangi
Whatu-ranga-nuku

Documented landing places of voyaging canoes

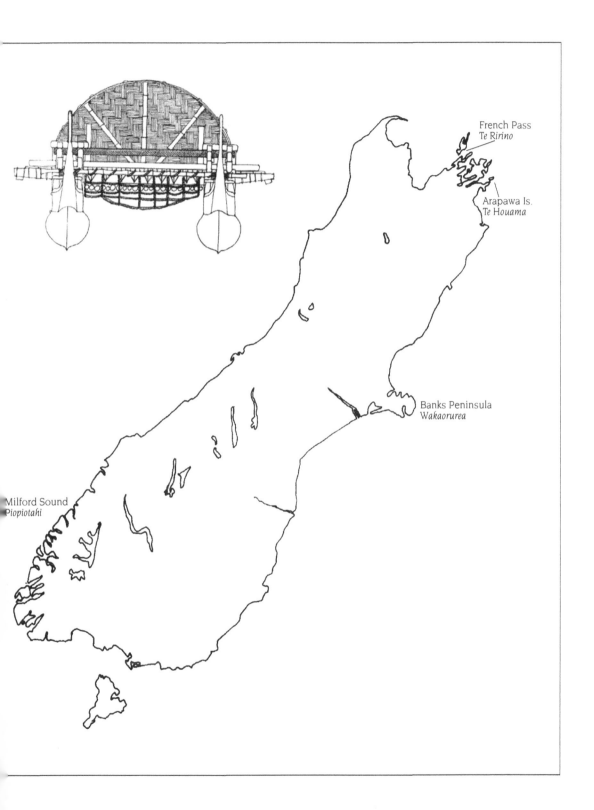

French Pass
Te Ririno

Arapawa Is.
Te Houama

Banks Peninsula
Wakaorurea

Milford Sound
Piopiotahi

KUPE'S VOYAGE TO AOTEAROA

Ka tito au, ka tito au,   I will sing, I will sing,
Ka tito au ki a Kupe,   I will sing of Kupe,
Te tangata nana i hoehoe te moana,   The man who paddled the ocean,
Te tangata nana i topetope te whenua,   The man who separated the land,
Tu ke a Kapiti, tu ke a Mana,   Solitary stands Kapiti, separated is Mana,
Tau ke a Arapaoa.   Removed is Arapaoa.
Ko nga tohu tena   Those are the signs
A toku tupuna a Kupe.   Of my ancestor Kupe.
Nana i whakatomene Titapua,   It was he who explored Titapua
Ka toreke i a au te whenua nei.   This land given up by me.[1]

How the islands of Aotearoa were discovered so far to the south of any inhabited islands is still a hotly debated topic. The most probable scenario is that the regular migration of the long-tailed cuckoo and bob-tailed godwit alerted the Polynesians to the probability of new lands to the south-west. Each year, as thousands of these birds flew from the cooler northern latitudes via the Central Pacific Islands, their habits would have been keenly observed. The Polynesians' in-depth knowledge of their natural habitat would have alerted them to the fact that the migrating birds were all land-based species, and would therefore need to nest on land during the months they were absent.

By noting the exact direction the flocks of birds took year after year in relation to setting stars and planets on the horizon, the precise co-ordinates for an expedition could be carefully charted.[2] All that would be needed was a well-provisioned, solid waka, an experienced crew, and a navigator who was

1. A traditional Maori waiata. Anne Nelson, *Nga Waka Maori*: 9.
2. As explained in the chapter on traditional navigation, the aligning of voyaging routes with rising or setting stars was the main technique employed by navigators to establish and fix direction.

Early voyagers to Aotearoa are thought to have followed the migration routes of godwits (above), long-tailed cuckoos (left) and other birds as they passed through the central and western Pacific during their annual migrations.

sufficiently skilled to make allowances for any drift caused by currents and storms that might take the waka off course, and by the grace of the gods the voyage would be successful.

By all accounts, the actual detection of the land mass of Aotearoa would probably have been one of the easiest finds in the history of Polynesian island discovery. The huge size of the island group, in particular its side-on length in relation to the direction of the explorers' approach, would have made it hard to miss. Men skilled in finding small atolls in the middle of the Pacific Ocean would have little trouble detecting these islands while still a fair distance from shore.

It is Kupe, explorer of the Pacific Ocean, Te Moana-nui-a-Kiwa, who is credited with voyaging deep into the southern ocean in his waka Matahourua and discovering the uninhabited island group now known as Aotearoa. Sailing further and further away from the tropical warmth of his

Pacific island homeland, Kupe voyaged where no one had been before, to the Land of the Long White Cloud. After resting his crew on the northern shores, Kupe is said to have sailed his waka along the rugged coastline exploring the uninhabited land, personally naming many spots along the way. Many of these bays and headlands are remembered in tradition, and are recalled later in this chapter. Having extensively voyaged around the North Island and along the west coast of the South Island, Kupe returned to his homeland to tell of his discovery, and to share the voyaging instructions with his fellow navigators.

The discovery of Aotearoa by Kupe is remembered in two quite different sagas. The first is recalled in 'the legend of Kupe', and differs significantly from 'the tradition of Kupe' that follows. The version of events passed down in 'the legend of Kupe' is perhaps comparable to the Carolinian aruruwow. In this ancient system from the Caroline Islands, navigational information is passed between navigators via a simple story. These stories are often told and retold by non-navigators purely for their beauty, and the uninitiated usually have no knowledge of the important information contained within.

An example of an aruruwow is given in Stephen Thomas's *The Last Navigator*. It tells of an uru, or parrot fish, hiding in its hole in a reef that surrounds an island. A fisherman tries to net the fish, which evades him and swims to a reef at another island. Again the fisherman attempts to catch the fish in his dip net, and once again the fish escapes, this time to a third reef. Each time the fish reaches the sanctuary of another reef, the storyteller refers to the reef by a name that only those with prior knowledge will recognise, and thus the specific details of the course are passed on.

Other navigational information could also be passed on in story form. In Sir Arthur Grimble's *Migrations, Myth and Magic from the Gilbert Islands*, we learn how the tale of a popular mythical hero is used to bind together sailing directions to help navigators memorise them.[3]

In the example given, it is explained that the hero has just commenced a journey:

> when he comes across an old woman sitting in the door of her house (a figurative description of the star cluster Pleiades), on whom he played some familiar trick which causes her to flee westward (towards the setting sun). Later he meets a man sailing his canoe from the east (similar to the cross section of a canoe, this refers to the V-shape in the constellation Taurus, featuring the star Aldebaran). The two talk until the old woman falls into the sea (Pleiades sets), making such a hideous noise as she disappears, that the hero runs away to the east and takes refuge with two old lepers (the sailing course changes to head towards Gemini).

3. Sir Arthur Grimble, *Migrations, Myth and Magic from the Gilbert Islands*: 218.

The example stops there, but it is obvious how such stories would act as aids to memorising the instructions for reaching a particular destination. Grimble goes on to note that these stories are usually incredibly difficult to dissect, with each family using a different set of visual aids to help them remember the stars and constellations. He finishes by saying that star-lore was one of the most secret and guarded possessions held by any family.

The legend of Kupe

This version of Kupe's discovery of Aotearoa is woven around the story of Kupe and his fellow voyager, Ngahue, as they chase a giant octopus, Te Wheke-o-Muturangi, from their homeland to the shores of Aotearoa.

It is said that the cause of the voyage that led to the discovery of Aotearoa is to be laid at the feet of Muturangi and his pet octopus, Te Wheke-o-Muturangi. Te Wheke had many children who were in the habit of stealing the bait off the hooks of Kupe and his fellow tribesmen while they were out fishing in the open ocean. Despite Kupe's continual pleas, Muturangi refused to restrain his pet and her family, leaving Kupe and his kinsmen with no choice other than to take matters into their own hands.

It was determined by the village elders that for the good of the many people that relied on the fishermen's regular catch, Te Wheke-o-Muturangi and her children must be destroyed. A simple plan was decided upon and it was agreed that it would be implemented as soon as possible. Kupe himself was given the responsibility of killing Te Wheke.

The next morning, before first light, the fishermen set off from the village in their canoes, aiming to get to the fishing grounds before the sun came up. When they arrived, they lowered their anchors and carefully let down their fishing lines. Unbeknown to the octopuses, however, the fishermen hadn't lowered their lines as deep as usual, and so were able to detect the wheke as they wrapped their tentacles around the bait. By gently pulling up their lines, Kupe and his companions were able to raise the unsuspecting baby octopuses to the surface, where they slaughtered large numbers of them. Despite the distressing scene before her, Te Wheke kept her distance, giving Kupe no opportunity to attack her.

Later that night, after all the fishermen had returned to shore, another meeting of the villagers was called. It was decided by the elders that Kupe and Ngahue must prepare their waka, the Matahourua and the Tawirirangi respectively, to chase down Te Wheke and kill her. The next day, as Kupe completed the preparation of the waka, his wife, Hine-i-te-aparangi, called him aside. During the previous night she had had a premonition that he would die during the voyage, and she begged him to remain with her at Hawaiki. Furious that his wife would dare to shame him by asking him to neglect his duty to his kinsmen, Kupe ordered his wife and children to ready their personal provisions for the voyage. His punishment for her was that his entire family should sail with him to share in the unknown dangers that lay ahead.

The urgency of the mission was such that the usual custom of both waka leaving together was disregarded, and Ngahue set off in pursuit of the wheke as soon as his waka was ready. It wasn't long before he caught up with the unsuspecting wheke, but he was unable to attack her as she continued to swim just out of reach.

Despite Kupe's best efforts, it was a number of days before he was able to find the Tawirirangi and catch up with Ngahue. On being asked of the wheke's whereabouts, Ngahue responded by instructing Kupe to look deep into the ocean, where the red glow of the octopus was faintly visible. As the two waka chased the octopus further and further south into colder southern

Castle Point, where Te Wheke-o-Muturangi was cornered by Ngahue in the cave known as Te-Ana-o-Te-Wheke-o-Muturangi (the cave of Te Wheke-o-Muturangi).

seas, they entered a part of the ocean unknown to any of the men. Despite the days shortening and the nights becoming bitterly cold, the two crews continued their relentless chase southwards.

After what must have seemed like an eternity to the crews, land was finally sighted. Kupe's wife, Hine-i-te-aparangi, is credited with seeing the first sign of land: a huge, long, stationary cloud on the horizon. She is said to have exclaimed, 'He ao! He ao!' (A cloud! A cloud!) Legend states that it was from this exclamation that the name Aotearoa evolved (ao = cloud, tea = white, roa = long), commonly translated as Land of the Long White Cloud.

Once the two waka had successfully made landfall on the northern shores of Muriwhenua (Northland), the crews rested and fresh food was procured. Fish were plentiful in coastal waters, and birds sang in unrivalled abundance in the forest. The two captains agreed that Ngahue and the Tawirirangi would continue to follow Te Wheke as she continued south along the east coast, while Kupe and his crew would explore the west coast. Should Ngahue manage to corner the beast, he was instructed to keep her trapped and await Kupe's arrival.

While the Matahourua was sailed down the west coast of Te Ika a Maui (the North Island), with Kupe carefully taking note of the terrain and looking for signs of inhabitants, Ngahue managed to corner Te Wheke at Rangi-whakaoma (Castle Point), where the octopus was sheltering in a cave (subsequently named Te Ana-o-Te-Wheke-o-Muturangi, the cave of Te Wheke-o-Muturangi). Unable to leave the cave with the crew of the Tawirirangi waiting outside, the giant octopus rested and waited, all the while regaining her strength.

This is how Kupe found things when he finally arrived. The two chiefs conferred and planned their attack. It was agreed that Kupe would attack Te Wheke by himself, hoping to out-manoeuvre the beast in the confined space of the cave. Despite Kupe's cautious approach, Te Wheke was waiting for him as he entered her lair. Fighting desperately for her life, Te Wheke was able to defend herself as Kupe repeatedly attacked her, and eventually managed to escape from the cave in the fading light. Once again the two crews had to turn and give chase.

Having rounded Te Kawakawa (Cape Palliser), the two waka followed the coast and eventually reached the mouth of an imposing harbour. After familiarising himself with the local conditions, Kupe ordered the expedition into Whanganui-a-Tara (Wellington Harbour). While the crews spent time in the shelter of the harbour, they checked their waka for signs of wear and tear, and gathered food for the upcoming journey. Kupe, confident that the octopus would not be able to get too far away from them despite the un-familiar surroundings, let his men enjoy the warm weather during the start of the summer months.

After a lengthy rest the two waka parted company. The Tawirirangi sailed south to Te Wai Pounamu (the South Island) in search of Te Wheke, while Kupe sailed around to Porirua Harbour on the west coast. It is remembered that it was here that one of the Matahourua's anchors was replaced with a local boulder found on the eastern shore of the harbour.

From Porirua, Kupe sailed his waka to the nearby island of Mana, where Hine-i-te-aparangi and their daughters, Matiu, Makaro, Mohuia and Hine-te-uru, disembarked. He then rejoined the chase, sailing across Raukawa (Cook Strait) to join up with Ngahue. It wasn't long before the two waka once again caught up with the giant octopus, which was waiting for

Mana Island, named Te Mana-o-Kupe-ki-Aotearoa by Kupe in commemoration of his voyage.

them in the vicinity of Nga Whetu (The Brothers), an outcrop of rocks situated on the western side of Raukawa.

After the ordeal at Rangi-whakaoma, Te Wheke had become aggressive and now charged the two waka. As the octopus closed in on them, the two captains ordered their steersmen to veer out and widen the gap, allowing room to attack the monster as it swam between the waka. Tohirangi from the Matahourua and Ngahue both threw spears at Te Wheke, but to little effect. The octopus, enraged even more, turned and grabbed hold of the canoes with its gigantic tentacles. As she thrashed about, Kupe began to hack at her with his adze, Ranga-tu-whenua. Despite losing several of her tentacles, Te Wheke held fast to the two waka. In desperation, Kupe ordered Po-heuea to distract the octopus by throwing some calabashes at her head. With Te Wheke fooled into thinking she was being attacked by a number of men in the water, Kupe was able to take advantage and with one fierce strike to her head from his adze, managed to kill her.

Immediately after the epic struggle, a karakia was said at the spot where Te Wheke was finally killed. The two captains then made plans for the remainder of the voyage. It was decided that the two waka would continue on and explore the great southern land that lay ahead. The waka were sailed down the west coast of Te Wai Pounamu, landing at Arahura, where pounamu (greenstone) was found. Ngahue is also said to have killed a number of moa in the area and preserved the meat to take back to Hawaiki.

Voyaging north again, the two waka sailed to Mana Island, where Kupe was reunited with his family, before completing the voyage to the northern harbour of Hokianga. From Hokianga the two waka are said to have returned directly to Hawaiki.

If this was originally the equivalent of an aruruwow (and it is by no means certain that it is), it is probable that most of the navigational information is missing from the version that survives today. Whether this is because those with the sacred knowledge chose not to pass it on to the Pakeha collectors of tales, or because the relevant information was slowly filtered out unintentionally by non-navigators, is now not known.

The tradition of Kupe

This version of the story of the discovery of Aotearoa is considered by some to portray a more realistic chronicle of events, and starts with the building of two waka, the Matahourua and the Aotea, in Hawaiki.

It is remembered that on the banks of the river Awa-nui-a-rangi stood a huge tree that had two well-formed trunks. Toto, a man with considerable mana in his district, had claimed ownership of the tree years before, judging it to possess excellent qualities for shaping into canoe hulls. Finally the day came to fell the mighty tree. It was decided that two waka were to be constructed from the tree, one each for Toto's daughters, Rongorongo and Kura-maro-tini. The waka were to be used as wedding gifts for the girls' prospective husbands. Toto called upon Kauika and Turi-ua-nui to build Rongorongo's waka, which was to be named Aotea, while Kupe was asked to oversee the construction of the Matahourua for Kura-maro-tini.

Once the appropriate karakia had been recited and the felling ceremony completed, the construction of the waka commenced. With the resources made available to the workmen by their benefactor, Toto, the waka were beautifully built to the highest standards.

Not long after the two waka were completed, Toto decided that Rongorongo and Kura-maro-tini were ready to be married. It was agreed that Rongorongo would marry Turi, while Kura-maro-tini was to marry Hoturapa. It was clear to Kupe, however, that Kura-maro-tini was more interested in him than Hoturapa, and he formed a plan to eliminate Kura-maro-tini's prospective husband. He began by secretly preparing the Matahourua for an ocean voyage, collecting together enough provisions for a long trip, and then managed to convince some of his trusted friends to act as crew for him. Next, he arranged with Kura-maro-tini that she meet him near the Matahourua later that night. Finally, he talked the unsuspecting Hoturapa into joining him in a deep-sea fishing expedition.

As the two fishermen paddled out into the open ocean they talked amicably. Kupe, ever careful not to betray any sign of the deceit swelling within his chest, acted like a close friend. Once they were sufficiently far out, Kupe cast the anchor over the side of his fishing waka. As Hoturapa readied his fishing line, Kupe secretly began to recite a karakia to ensure that the anchor would be impossible to haul up later in the day.

As the day wore on, the canoe began to fill with the abundance of fish caught in the rich seas that surrounded the fishermen's Pacific homeland. When the sun neared the western horizon, Kupe suggested to his companion that they should return to their village before the night overtook them. Hoturapa agreed, and the pair of them pulled up their fishing lines. Once the lines were in and their fish secured, Kupe called to Hoturapa that the anchor was stuck, perhaps on a reef, and would he dive down to free it. Hoturapa readily agreed to try and free the anchor, and dived into the warm ocean. When Hoturapa was well under the ocean surface and still following the anchor rope down into the depths, the devious Kupe severed the rope and began to paddle back to his village. He had abandoned Hoturapa to die in the arms of Tangaroa, guardian of the ocean.

Seeing the rope go limp, but not yet realising the horrible truth, Hoturapa swam back up to the surface. As soon as he resurfaced, Hoturapa looked about for the waka, only to see it speeding off towards land. He called to Kupe, pleading with him to return and pick him up. To his utter disbelief Kupe ignored his pleas and continued paddling towards shore. Fortunately for Hoturapa, one of the guardians of the ocean, Rangi-uru-hinga, saw the entire incident and decided to help Hoturapa return to shore. Despite Rangi-uru-hinga's assistance, however, Hoturapa was unable to reach the village before Kura-maro-tini, Kupe and his hand-picked crew departed again aboard the Matahourua.

The course set by Reti, navigator of the waka,[4] was to follow a star path that would correspond closely with the position of the setting sun. By sailing towards the point on the horizon where a steady stream of preselected stars set — a little to the left of this one, a little to the right of that one — the waka was held on its course. During the day the constant and even swell of the ocean ensured that, should the waka go off course, the changing roll of the waka would alert the navigator immediately.

All is remembered as having gone well during the voyage until the waka reached a place named Raro-pouriuri, where Kupe sensed that the waka was being followed. His intuition proved to be correct, and the nets of Kahukura, named Tupua-horo-nuku and Tai-horo-nuku-rangi, were encountered. These nets were sent by Kupe's adversaries Kiwa and Kama to pursue him and force him to return to Hawaiki. It wasn't until Kupe sacrificed two of his crew, Te Tuhi-o-te-po and Rangi-riri, to the sea that he managed to escape Kiwa and Kama. The two men changed into taniwha immediately upon entering the ocean and guided the Matahourua to safety.

---

4. It is not commonly known, but it is said in some versions of the tradition that there was a second navigator on the Matahourua, named Reti. It is not clear whether Kupe or Reti was the primary navigator of the expedition. It is noted elsewhere in this book that Polynesians sometimes had two navigators on a waka, to share the workload and as a safeguard against disaster should one perish during the voyage.

Further on in the voyage, Kupe discovered a small uninhabited island which was subsequently named Wawau-atea-nui. It is possible that this was one of the islands in the Kermadec chain, as it was said to be three days' sailing from Aotearoa.

When Kupe did arrive in Aotearoa, his first landfall was at Whangaroa, where an underwater phenomenon called Te-au-kanapanapa (bright or gleaming current)[5] guided him to land. From Whangaroa, Kupe went on to explore his new land.

The following places, sourced from both legend and the tradition and arranged alphabetically, are remembered as having been visited by Kupe.

Makaro	Ward Island
Mana Island	The well-known island out from Porirua Harbour. Kupe named it Te Mana-o-Kupe-ki-Aotearoa to commemorate his successful crossing of Te Moana-nui-a-Kiwa (the Pacific Ocean).

5. Te-au-kanapanapa is described as 'underwater lightning' and is still reported as being seen, usually about 2 m under the ocean surface. This sign is well known in other parts of the Pacific as an aid in finding islands and atolls, and shows itself as flashes of light that emanate from land.

Matakitaki	A large rock on the east side of Palliser Bay, where Kupe stood looking at Te Wai Pounamu. Near the rock is a pool of water which is red, supposedly from the blood of his daughters, who are said to have cut themselves when Kupe left them there. Another source claims Matakitaki to be the original name of the northern summit of Mana Island.
Matiu	Formerly called Somes Island.
Mo-huia	A rock in the vicinity of Sinclair Head.
Nga Kuri-a-Kupe	A rock on the east side of the Whirinaki River mouth, which is said to be in the shape of Kupe's dogs.
Nga-ra-o-Kupe	Two triangular, light-coloured patches surrounded by green vegetation to the west of Cape Palliser. (Literally: the sails of Kupe.)
Nga-tauari-a-Matahourua	A spot 6 km south-east of the mouth of the Wairau River, on the bluff called Pari-nui-a-whiti, and now known as White Bluff. (Literally: the thwarts of the Matahourua.)
Nga-waka-a-Kupe	The range of hills known as Aorangi above Cape Palliser. Also a group of rocks in Admiralty Bay. (Literally: the waka [plural] of Kupe.)
Pari-Whero	Red Rocks Point, near Sinclair Head. There are two traditions explaining the naming of this spot. The first claims Kupe's daughters caused the rocks to turn red when they began to cut themselves as a sign of mourning, believing Kupe to be dead. According to the second, Kupe cut his own hand on a paua shell while collecting seafood.

Rangiora Point

A place where one of the waka's anchors is said to rest, on the west side of The Narrows, Hokianga.

Taonui-o-Kupe

A spot at Jacksons Head, Queen Charlotte Sound. Kupe is said to have unsuccessfully thrown his taonui (a kind of spear) at this point from the North Island.

Te Kakau-o-te-toki-a-Kupe

A rock on Te-uira-ka-rapa Point in Tory Channel, opposite Moioio Island. (Literally: the handle of the adze of Kupe.)

Te Kawakawa

Cape Palliser, where a daughter of Kupe made a wreath of kawakawa leaves.

Te Kohukohu

One of Matahoura's bailers was turned to stone near this Hokianga landmark.

Te Koko-a-Kupe

A place in Cloudy Bay.

Te Kupenga-a-Kupe

Also in the vicinity of Jacksons Head. (Literally: Kupe's net.)

Te Mimi-o-Kupe

A place in the vicinity of Tory Channel.

Te Punga-o-Mata-hourua

A spot near Paremata where an anchor of the Matahourua was discarded. (Literally: the anchor of Matahourua.)

Te Puru

Kupe is said to have left a stone here, somewhere in the Upper Waihou River system. Maori in the know chant a karakia when passing the spot to protect themselves, and place a few cuttings from a karamu or kawakawa tree, or pebbles they have brought along for that purpose. Once they have made their offering and are departing, they take care not to look back.

Te-ra-o-Mata-hourua

A place near Ohariu, on the coast west of Wellington. (Literally: the sail of Matahourua.) The same sail is also said to have been dried at Hataitai Beach or Lyall Bay.

Te Rimurapa	Sinclair Head, where bull-kelp was collected and made into bags for preserving food.
Te Tangihanga-a-Kupe (Te Raranga-a-Kupe)	Barretts Reef. Kupe is said to have cried at this point when he left his daughters near Matakitaki (see page 40). A second name for this reef is Te Raranga-a-Kupe.
Te Tou-o-Puraho	Another of the Matahourua's bailers was turned to stone here, near Te Whakarara-a-Kupe (see below).
Te Turanga-a-Kupe	The foreshore at Seatoun, near Pinnacle Rock.
Te Ure-o-Kupe (Te Aroaro-o-Kupe)	One of the pointed rocks on Barretts Reef, at the entrance to Wellington Harbour. This rock is also known as Te Aroaro-o-Kupe. (Literally: the penis of Kupe.)
Te Whakarara-a-Kupe	A spot at Tara-roto-rua, between Kerikeri and Whangaroa, where Kupe arranged a feast. It is claimed that Kupe used stones to display the food instead of the customary boards supported by poles.
Toka-haere	A rock near Sinclair Head.
Wai-tawa	A landing place of the Matahourua, just inside the Porirua heads, on the south side.
Wharo	A place north of Hokianga on the coast. Kupe's footprints are said to be indented in rock there.

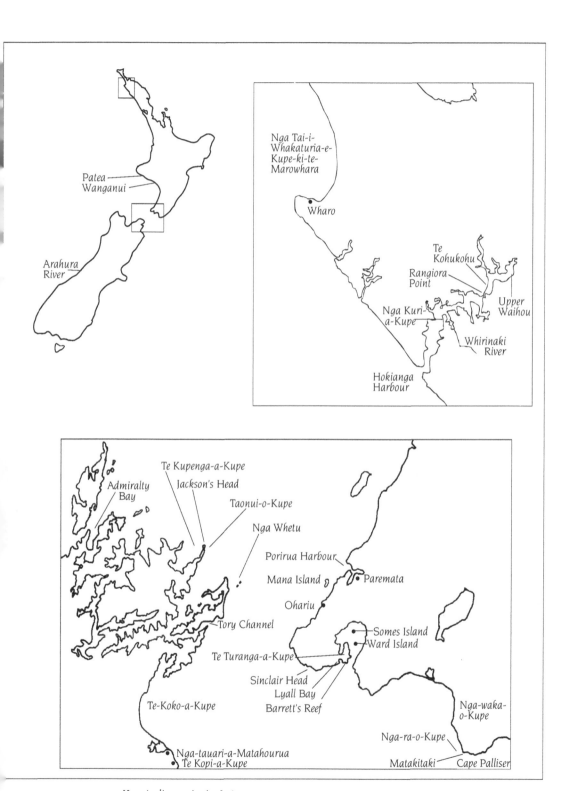

Kupe's discoveries in Aotearoa

After the exhaustive voyage of exploration around Te Ika a Maui, and a large portion of the west coast of Te Wai Pounamu, Kupe returned to the west coast of Te Ika a Maui, from where he began to venture northwards. Along the way, Kupe ordered a further rest for the crews at Whanganui, where the district was given the name Kaihau-o-Kupe. It is said that the name was given because of the constant strong winds encountered there. A little further north, up the coast at Patea, Kupe went ashore again, this time to smell and feel the soil. He judged that crops would grow well in the rich, moist earth. From the Taranaki district the expedition continued north before stopping again, this time at Hoki-anga-nui (Hokianga Harbour).

Not long after settling down in the beautiful surroundings of Hoki-anga-nui, Kupe began to yearn for his homeland of Hawaiki, probably wishing to see out his days in the company of friends and a familiar setting. As he began to prepare for the return voyage, he knew in the back of his mind that he would need to make a significant offering to the gods if he wanted to count on them to protect his waka during the upcoming journey. With a heavy heart Kupe concluded that it must be his own son, Tuputupu-whenua, who must be sacrificed if the gods were to be fully appeased. First Kupe cast a hirihiri (a type of spell) over Tuputupu-whenua, and then he placed him in the spring named Te Puna-i-te-ao-marama. (Legend says that Tuputupu-whenua is still to be found in the spring to this day.) His offering to the gods was completed with the appropriate karakia.

Hoki-anga-nui (Hokianga Harbour) where Kupe is said to have settled before returning to Hawaiki

Once all the preparations for the voyage had been completed and the waka readied, Kupe addressed his crew, giving them the choice of staying in Aotearoa or returning with him to Hawaiki. A number decided to stay in this new land despite its cooler climate and rugged landscape. When asked by those who chose to remain behind whether he would ever return to Aotearoa, Kupe replied, 'E hoki Kupe?' This has since become a famous saying, and is still used to say 'no' politely.

Those remembered from the crew from Kupe's village in the traditional version are:

Kupe	Kura-maro-tini	Reti (the navigator)
Te Mauru	Ripi-i-roa-iti	Rua-rangi
Tirairaka	Te Tuhi-o-te-po	Makaro
Wai-ehua	Te Rangi-pouri	Tupu-te-uru-roa
Kahu-nui	Rangi-riri	Tuputupu-whenua
Tama-ki-hikurangi	Tamatea-uri-haere	Pari-i-Tane
Whauri	Matino	Tutu-mai-ao
Pari-ka-rangaranga	Tunga	Weta
Po-kohu	Moko-roa	

A number of others were picked up during the voyage from Hawaiki. The following are said to have been picked up at Nui-o-whiti, which is apparently at a place remembered as Pikopiko-i-whiti or Nui-o-wara:

Tutei	Karere
Pou-poto	Karihi
Pohe-te-ngu (Poho-te-ngu)	Turehu

From tribe to tribe there are minor variations in these two accounts of Kupe's story. Despite these differences, each version has validity and holds particular significance for the tribe to whom it belongs.

This notwithstanding, comparing the two main accounts of Kupe's voyage to Aotearoa does illustrate some fundamental differences. 'The tradition of Kupe' seems to be in line with many other Maori traditions of voyaging and migration — although the episode of Kahukura and his nets obstructing the progress of the Matahoura is unusual. By contrast, 'the legend of Kupe' appears to be the Polynesian equivalent of an aruruwow — an oral 'chart of the ocean'. The most obvious indication of this fact is the passage describing the two canoes following the red glow of the octopus Te Wheke-o-Muturangi deep in the ocean. If this glow were to be interpreted as the setting sun, then it would match the instruction commonly recalled in Maori lore of 'steering the canoes a little to the left of the setting sun' for the voyage to Aotearoa.

TALK OF THE NAVIGATORS

In looking for examples of Maori navigational lore, we are forced to search through the many traditions, karakia and waiata that have been passed down over the centuries. As we will see, much of the navigation information is hidden within the migration traditions, and is often only referred to in passing. There are a few star lists, a number of references to the moon, the sun and Venus as guiding bodies, but no complete sets of navigational instructions as such. Although we cannot hope to learn where the ancestors of the Maori voyaged from, when we read the surviving snippets of navigational knowledge we can gain a valuable insight into how information was 'stored' and passed on in the oral societies of Polynesia.

In recent times attempts have been made to recreate the voyages from Rarotonga to Aotearoa. The experience gained by the likes of David Lewis and more recently the navigators of a number of contemporary waka, including Hawaiki-nui and Te Aurere, is slowly helping to recover the navigational knowledge that has been eroded and lost over the centuries. We cannot know for certain how the ancient Polynesian seafarers navigated, but through practical trial and error it is possible to make qualified statements as to the most probable techniques used. It seems that for Polynesian navigation, this is our only door into the past.

Navigational information from Maori lore

Much of the original navigation lore of the Maori has been lost. What we have left is a collection of obscure references to gods and rainbows, men and taniwha, the sea and the stars. In an effort to decipher the hidden messages and discover 'the talk of the navigators', we need to delve into these traditions and search for clues behind the outer meaning.

As we have already noted, the Polynesians' stories of demi-gods and heroes performing super-human feats often had important information woven into their storylines, and were used to help remember details or instructions. One such figure is the pan-Polynesian Kahukura, who features in a number of Maori traditions in various roles. In the excerpts from traditions that are offered later in this chapter, he is variously named as a protecting god, who along with six other gods resided in the cave Te Kohurau; a god in the form of a solar rainbow; and an explorer who travelled to Aotearoa by way of a rainbow.

The examples that follow have all been found among the many recorded traditions, karakia and waiata telling the story of waka migrations. When reading through the traditions, it is evident that many important details are missing. Basic information, such as the names of certain stars and the time of year that particular waka embarked, is sometimes recorded, but more specific details, such as which significant island groups (the Kermadec Islands, for example) are encountered along the way, or where dangerous ocean currents might be encountered, are missing. Whether this knowledge was gradually lost over the centuries because it was no longer used, or deliberately left out when it was passed on to Europeans, is now unclear.

The following section, presented in alphabetical order by waka name, is a review of the navigational information encountered in Maori lore.

Aotea

From the tradition of the Aotea waka comes this small verse containing a reference to the star Rehua (Antares), which is suggested as the guiding star.

> Now the (course of the) canoe rests
> On the Tipua-o-te-rangi
> On Tawhito-o-te-rangi
> On the place of Rehua's eyes.

Several gods are also named as accompanying the Aotea on its voyage to Aotearoa: Maru, Te Ihinga-o-te-rangi, Kahukura, Rongomai, and Haere-iti. It should be noted that Kahukura and Rongomai both feature in a number of other traditions as well, including those of the Horouta and Takitimu.

Te Arawa

Ngatoroirangi is acknowledged as the navigator of Te Arawa. To quote tradition, it is said that he:

> understood the language of the stars, the children of the lord of light, Tane-nui-a-rangi; he conversed with the moon, Hinauri; and he kept the prow of Te Arawa pointed in a direction that was a little to the left of the setting sun.

As a seasoned navigator, Ngatoroirangi was acquainted with the prevailing winds of the seasons and the stars that were visible each month. He knew that when his ancestors sailed from the north to Hawaiki, new constellations and stars appeared over the horizon; and that when they reached the Pito-o-watea (equator) they lost sight of the North Star. The South Star, in the constellation of Humu,[1] would then appear as their guide. Ngatoroirangi also knew that southern voyages were carried out between December and March when the north-west trade wind was strongest. He also knew that Kupe's instructions for sailing from Rarotonga to Aotearoa included the advice to steer a little to the left of Venus in the month of February.

Another reference relating to the navigation of Te Arawa to Aotearoa says:

> *Kia whakatau koutou ki a Atutahi ma Rehua;*
> *ko Atutahi e whakatata nei ki te Mangaroa!*

> *Direct your course to Canopus by Antares;*
> *Canopus that is by the side of the Milky Way!*

Horouta

The following excerpt is from the tradition of the Horouta waka, and features Kahukura as both a man and part of a rainbow. This reference is of particular interest because the names are given in strict order: Hine-te-wai on the bottom, Rongomai above her, and so on. It is suggested that the names listed in Kahukura's rainbow could in fact be those of navigation stars, carefully remembered with the help of the rainbow.

> *Two men named Kahukura and Rongo-i-amo travelled to Aotearoa by way of a rainbow. The rainbow was constructed by several people standing in Hawaiki, and bending over so that their hands reached the North Island of Aotearoa, in the vicinity of Whakatane. It was this rainbow that the navigator of the Horouta is said to have followed during its voyage to Aotearoa.*

The rainbow constructed by Kahukura was made up with:

Hine-te-wai (Kahukura's mother, on the bottom)
Rongomai (Kahukura's father, on top of her)
Te Paoka-o-te-rangi (next)
Totoerangi (arched)
Kahukura (the man himself)
Tahawai
Kau-rukiruki
Here-umu

1. Humu features in Tongan astronomy as the Coal Sack, an empty area of space near the Southern Cross.

Another reference from Horouta tradition claims:

> ... the pilot of the canoe was Kahukura-i-te-rangi, who stood with one foot upon the ocean and the other upon the land, and when his face appears like an arch in the heavens, that is Kahukura bending down and behind him is his wife, Te Atua-wharoro-mai-te-rangi.

Mamari

The navigation instructions attributed to Kupe and passed on to Ruanui, the navigator of the Mamari, are of interest for two reasons. Firstly, they vary from the usual 'sail to the left of the setting sun' type that are commonly quoted; secondly, they refer to karakia for a sky rope and for the anchor of the waka. It is probable that the first karakia referred to for the sky rope contains the names of the navigation stars that rise from the distant horizon, one after the other, to be joined together in the navigator's mind by an imaginary rope. Likewise, it is plausible that the karakia for the anchor of the waka contains the star names for the return voyage to Hawaiki.

It is remembered that as a final word of advice to Ruanui before the departure, Kupe warned him:

> You must never forget the karakia for the sky rope, nor the one for the anchor of the canoe. If you do, you and all your people will surely perish...

> When you go, lay the bow of the canoe to the Cloud Pillar that lies south-west. When night falls, steer towards the star Atua-tahi. Hold to the left of Mangaroa (the Milky Way) and travel on. When day breaks, again sail towards the Cloud Pillar and continue on.

By following these instructions, Ruanui sailed the Mamari directly to Hokianga. Unfortunately, no record of either karakia seems to have survived.

It is also recorded that a number of taniwha accompanied the Mamari on its voyage: Arai-te-uru, Niua, Te Tohi-o-te-po and Kanapu-i-te-rangi. The god Tohi-nui-a-rangi, said to live in the rising moon, was also sent to watch over the waka as it sailed south to the new land.

Matahourua

Little detail is recorded about the navigation of the Matahourua to Aotearoa, other than that the waka is said to have been sailed on the path of the sun until it reached a place named Raro-pouriuri. It was here that Kupe noticed that the waka was being chased by Tupua-horo-nuku and Tai-horo-nuku-rangi — the nets of Kahukura. These were sent by Kiwa and Kama to pursue Kupe. In a desperate attempt to escape, Kupe had two of his crew, Te Tuhi-o-te-po and Rangi-riri, thrown into the sea as sacrifices. They immediately became guiding taniwha and helped Kupe to elude his pursuers.

It is interesting to note that in Anutan star lore, the Southern Cross is known as Te Kupenga (the net). This may be another case of an everyday object being used in a story to remind the navigator of a star or constellation.

Tainui

The following extract comes from Best's *The Astronomical Knowledge of the Maori*, and is of particular interest if you read it alongside the discussion of star lore at the end of this chapter for the voyage of the Hokule'a to Aotearoa, where the same stars and constellations feature.[2]

> *Te Ra o Tainui: Mr White gives this as the name of a star or constellation. In his unpublished MS. [manuscript] he gives a diagram of the Tainui canoe as represented by stars. The Pleiades form the bow of the starry vessel, and the three bright stars in Orion's belt represent the stern. The sail, Te Ra o Tainui, is perhaps the Hyades. The cable is seen as The Pointers, and the anchor is Te Punga a Tama-rereti, the Southern Cross.*

Takitimu

There are probably more navigation stars associated with the Takitimu in traditions than for any other waka. This comprehensive list of ten stars and constellations agrees with the contemporary Micronesian view that ten to twelve stars would usually be sufficient for a night's navigation:

Atutahi	Canopus
Tautoru	Orion's belt
Puanga	Rigel
Karewa	Unknown
Takurua Sirius	
Tawera	Venus as Morning Star
Meremere	Venus as Evening Star
Matariki	Pleiades
Tama-rereti	Possibly the tail of Scorpius
Te Ika-roa	The Galaxy or Milky Way

Another tradition also names Wero-i-te-ninihi as one of the stars used for nightly observations at sea.

Following are the names given for gods and guardians of the Takitimu, which give a full account of the names associated with the voyage.

Gods:	Io and Ha
Lesser gods:	Kahukura, Tama-i-waho, Motipua, Tu-nui-o-te-ika, Tu-korako, Te Po-tua-tini, Hine-pukohu-rangi,

2. Elsdon Best, *The Astronomical Knowledge of the Maori*: 60.

	Tahaia, Tukopiri, Te Whanuapo, Tara-kumukumu, Poro-hinaki
Guardians of the ocean:	Ruamano, Arai-te-uru, Tutara-kauika, Houmea, Te Petipeti, Te Ranga-hua, Tai-mounu, Tane Rakahia

Another list of protecting gods remembered is: Kahukura, Tama-i-waho, Tunui-o-te-ika, Hine-korako, Rongomai, Tuhinapo and Ruamako. These seven gods were said to reside in the cave known as Te Kohurau. Could Te Kohurau be the name of the star path or star pit for the navigation stars?

In light of the need to use stars irregularly spaced about the horizon (as described in the voyage of the Hokule'a), the reference to taniwha swimming in front of, to the side of and behind the Takitimu in the next entry may lend further strength to the argument that some of the taniwha named in this tradition could be the names of navigation stars.

During the voyage of the Takitimu, the god Kahukura (in the form of a solar rainbow), was sent ahead by day to guide the waka, while Hine-korako (in the form of a lunar rainbow), was sent at night. In the ocean Ruamano led the way, with Arai-te-uru following in the wake, and Tutara-kauika and Wehenga-kauki on either side. Tu-nui-o-te-ika is said to have been a messenger who reported the proximity of any land.

To conclude the notes associated with Takitimu and its voyage, we have the well-recorded but very general instructions:[3]

> Kia pai te takoto ihu o te waka i runga i a Kopu i te po;
> i te awatea ka whai i muri i a Tama-nui-te-ra.

> Keep the bow of the vessel carefully on Venus during the night
> and during daylight follow behind Tama-nui-te-ra, the sun.

Uruao

This entry for the waka Uruao mentions a number of stars that are said to have been used by the Polynesians of old to forecast the weather. It also mentions the habit of reciting karakia at night and the use of rainbows to guide the waka by day.

Before leaving Hawaiki, Matiti, navigator of the Uruao, is said to have visited Takopa at Tautari-nui-o-Matariki to learn the lore of the stars. He was told the stars Wero-i-te-ninihi, Wero-i-te-kokoto and Wero-i-te-aumaria portended a season of fair weather and signalled an ideal time for voyaging. During the long voyage south, it is recorded that the people on board recited karakia at night, and each morning rainbows would appear to point the way to their destination.

3. Best: 16.

Huruhurumanu, Kurahaupo and Rangimatoro

It is remembered that during the voyage of the Huruhurumanu to Aotearoa, the crew met 50 gigantic seas that threatened to swamp their waka. The guardian spirit of the waka was Tu-kai-tauru (Tu-kai-te-uru), who is also said to have been the guiding deity of the Kurahaupo and Rangimatoro. Tu-kai-tauru's prominence in three separate traditions indicates that this is possibly also the name of another guiding star.

The only other clue found in the Rangimatoro tradition is in the names of the chiefs and crew. It may be a coincidence, but the majority of those remembered have Rangi as part of their name (Rangi = sky or heavens). Perhaps these 'men' were also in fact the guiding stars. Chiefs on board were Hape-ki-tu-matangi-o-te-rangi (Hape-ki-tu-manui-o-te-rangi), Tau-ira-a-rangi, and Puhi-moenga-ariki. Crew on board included Te Hoka-o-te-rangi and Tikitiki-o-te-rangi.

Additional information

These next few entries are not identified with any particular waka, but have been added to enrich the information available for anyone wishing to explore this subject further. The following excerpt from an old oriori (a chant often used as a lullaby) mentions a number of stars linked with voyaging and weather forecasting (these are indicated in bold):

> E *hokai ana koe ki whea, e Tane-tikitiki ... e*
> Ka pa mai te waha — Ki te whai atu i taua nei puhi, e hika ... e
> E *hoki: Tangaroa e koe i nga tupuni o Wehi-nui-o-mamao*
> Ko Hihira ki uta, ko Hihira ki tai
> Ko Parinuku, ko Parirangi
> Tikina e koe ki te kahui whatu punga ... e
> Ko **Takurua** nei, e, **Meremere** nei, e, **Atutahi-ma-Rehua** nei ... e
> He ariki no te tau ka wehe nei ... e
> Ka tau mai ko Whakaneke-pungarehu nei ... e
> Ko Uaki-motumotu nei ... e
> Hei tupa i a **Wero-i-te-ninihi**, e, ko **Wero-i-te-kokota** nei ... e
> Ka puta i konei o raua tuahine
> A **Wero-i-te-marie**, a **Wero-i-te-ahuru** ... e
> Koia te wero i te mahana ... e
> Itataia ki te poho o Ranginui
> Koia Tama-nui-te-ra, e hine ... e
> Ka *haere wareware atu na koe ... e*
> Koia i tau ai te haere i te aoturoa, e hine ... e ... i
> E *hine aku ... e ... i.*

This next extract adds the Smaller Magellanic Cloud to the list of navigation aids available to the ancient Polynesian navigators.

The brow of Antares is upthrust in the heavens,
Canopus rises, Orion's belt is on high,
And I hold fast to the Smaller Magellanic Cloud.
The moon rises on the horizon and I set out.

Finally, here is yet another reference to the sailing instructions attributed to Kupe. It is of particular interest because during Hawaiki-nui's successful 1985 voyage from Tahiti to Aotearoa, the rising and setting positions of the sun and Venus, along with the positions of the Southern Cross as it moved across the heavens, were the mainstays of the navigating system used by the crew — although they sailed to the left of the setting sun.

Let it be to the right of the setting Sun, or the Moon, or Venus. But it must be during Orongo-nui, or the summer, in the Kaupeka o Tatau-uru-ora (month of November). Which is the very best part of the land? Leave the course in the current of Pareweranui (or Tahu-para-wera-nui).

Contemporary information

Rehu Moana

The following observation was recorded by David Lewis during his 1965 voyage from Rarotonga to Aotearoa in his catamaran, Rehu Moana, and lists the main stars noted by him.

The course was one hand span to the left of the setting sun, two thirds of a span left of Venus. Before Venus set, the Pleiades rose astern, followed as the night wore on by Bellatrix, Procyon, and Castor and Pollux in turn. Towards the morning the Pointers and the Southern Cross were abeam to port ...

Hokule'a

The following excerpt from the review by navigator Nainoa Thompson of the voyage to Aotearoa by the contemporary Hawaiian waka Hokule'a presents a comprehensive account of the conditions that Polynesians of old may have faced when sailing from Central Polynesia. The stars named are also very significant when compared to the section on the waka Tainui. In that entry, the Pleiades, Orion's belt, the Pointers and the Southern Cross are all included in the list of principal navigational aids.

Nainoa found that during the traditional voyaging period of mid-November through to mid- to late December there are few prominent stars that set in the south-west (the direction a waka faces when sailing to Aotearoa from the Central Pacific). The only option for him was to use stars behind and to the side of the waka. Matariki (The Pleiades) was used as it rose from the horizon directly behind the waka, while the three stars that make up the Belt of Orion were also used while low in the sky. Other stars and constellations employed in the navigation were The Southern Cross and The Pointers.

In practice, Nainoa was forced to align the Southern Cross or the Pointers with part of the rigging when he needed to use them for navigating. He had constantly to make allowances for the constellation's journey as the night wore on. While the search for appropriate navigating stars was an ongoing task, the crew unexpectedly encountered a large amount of cloud during the voyage. At one stage this forced Nainoa to steer by the Magellanic Clouds after all of his other options were obscured.

Hawaiki-nui

The following passage is an excerpt taken from the extended interview with waka builder Matahi Brightwell, which comprises part two of this book. The voyage of the waka Hawaiki-nui took the crew of five from Tahiti to Moorea, on to Ra'iatea, then to Rarotonga, and finally to Aotearoa.

During the voyage from Rarotonga to Aotearoa, Venus was one of our primary navigation aids. When we left Rarotonga, Venus was rising on our starboard stern-post and setting over the port bow. Approaching the middle of the night, when it was at its zenith, Venus sat on the edge of the sail. Initially we could use it throughout the night to guide us as it moved diagonally over us, but because Venus rises from a slightly different point on the horizon each night, we had to do a bit of mental juggling to adjust our course in relation to it later in the voyage.

Even so, it seemed a fail-safe system. While we were taking our main direction from Venus, we also had the Southern Cross to our port side, always pointing down towards Aotearoa. If we went off course it didn't take too long to realise it. Suddenly Venus disappeared from the rigging and the Southern Cross was no longer in place to our left. It was really like we had a narrow corridor to sail down.

We also knew that we were likely to encounter little cloud cover to obstruct our view of the heavens during November and December. As it turned out, there were very few nights when we didn't get at least a glimpse of the stars every couple of hours or so, although it was usually clear for most of the night. On the odd occasion when the stars weren't visible for long periods at a time, we were able to steer by using our streamers and the consistency of the wind's direction during the hours of darkness. We also had the rope out behind us as an additional aid.

Throughout these various traditions, it is remarkable how frequently individual stars are named. In oral history, waiata and karakia, stars like Antares, Canopus and Sirius, along with Orion's belt, Venus and the Milky Way, are repeatedly identified as navigational aids for the voyage to Aotearoa. Their incidence highlights the precision exercised by Polynesian navigators.

TRADITIONAL POLYNESIAN NAVIGATION

Despite the best efforts of David Lewis, Ben Finney and a host of other twentieth-century researchers and collectors of Pacific navigation lore, the majority of traditional Polynesian navigation knowledge has been lost through neglect since the introduction of European sailing techniques and technology two to three hundred years ago.

To help put the few remaining pieces of the jigsaw into place, it is useful to study the traditional methods still employed by modern-day Micronesian navigators. By comparing the small bits of information we have about Polynesian navigation with seemingly similar Micronesian techniques, we can begin to build up a composite picture of how the Polynesians may have navigated during the voyages from the Central Pacific to Aotearoa.

Before presenting this comparison, we will start by exploring how novice navigators are taught their art.

The education of navigators

The knowledge accumulated by a navigator was derived from years of training and experience, and was built up over generations by skilled men before him. In many islands throughout the Pacific, navigational knowledge was the property of certain families. For these families it was a jealously guarded gift passed down to them by their ancestors, and the information was kept secret from non-navigators and rival navigation schools alike.

Because of this, the majority of young men were taught by older family members, either their father, uncle or grandfather. It was rare for a young man to be taught by anyone outside this group, although under special circumstances, such as the untimely death of a father or uncle, arrangements could sometimes be made for a boy to study with a non-related navigator.

Informal tuition would typically start at an early age as the child sat with the men in the canoe sheds and listened to their stories and discussions. When the time was judged right by the village elders, formal training would commence for those boys thought to have the potential to become navigators. Initially the young men would learn of the stars and their places in the navigation system, including the exact positions that certain stars would rise and set around the horizon. Additionally, they would begin to memorise the many star courses to and from the known island world they lived in.

In Kiribati (formerly known as the Gilbert Islands), these first lessons were primarily taught in the maneaba, or meeting house. Instruction utilised the roof of the maneaba, which was sectioned off by the rafters and supporting beams for the thatching. The ridge-pole was supported by three rafters on each side, and the student was taught to imagine the roof as a number of individual sections, each representing a corresponding segment in the night sky. The spot where the northern rafters joined with the ridge-pole represented the Pleiades at its meridian[1] (24° north), the central apex indicated Rigel at its meridian (approximately 8° south), while the intersection of the southern rafters showed where Antares met its meridian (26° south). Added to these three rafters were a number of other poles that further divided the roof, or night sky.

Sitting at the base of the central supporting pillar for the roof below Rigel's apex and facing towards the eastern sky, the student began by learning the stars in Rigel's section of the sky, before moving on to the sections containing the Pleiades and Antares. The position of each star in the navigator's repertoire was learnt in relation to the eaves (horizon) for each season, at sunrise and sunset. It was common for a boy to have to recite the names and positions of over 170 stars to pass this part of his education. Although the stars were separated by poles on the underside of the maneaba's roof, the student was keenly aware of the relationship between different sections.

Once all the important stars were well and truly ingrained in his memory, the student could commence learning the star paths between the many islands. This information was also passed on in the maneaba, often with the help of a story involving a mythological hero.

In the Caroline Islands, the same type of information was taught in the men's house, but with the help of stones or pieces of coral about a mat rather than rafters on the roof. As in Kiribati, the instruction began with learning the names of the most important stars, along with their rising and setting horizon points. These horizon points were then indicated with stones in a circle about the mat to test the student's knowledge. Next, the student had to master the names of all of the stars that would lie over the outrigger, stern and lee platform of his waka when he was sailing in any given direction. Further instruction related other aspects of star lore, all of which the student would have to master before he could hope to venture onto the ocean to continue his training.

1. A star's meridian is its highest apparent point in the sky when viewed from the earth.

While learning the star courses between the islands, the student would also learn about conditions likely to have an effect on the progress of a waka during a voyage. This information included currents expected on each leg of a voyage, how to read the many signs available from the swell and waves, forecasting the weather, judging drift in storms, and the emergency courses to nearby islands should a planned journey need to be abandoned for any reason.

The exact approach taught for individual navigational problems, such as confirming the direction of land while it is still out of sight, varied between schools throughout the Pacific. To a large extent, any individual solution depended on the natural environment for each island, and how the preceding generations had managed to 'read' that environment. While one island may have been blessed with an abundance of bird life that could be relied upon to guide a waka to land, another may have been virtually barren of birds. After generations of trial and error, the navigators from the latter island may have decided that reading the reflection and refraction of ocean swells was the most reliable technique for finding land.[2]

An important aid in helping navigators memorise the hundreds of facts needed for their trade were the stories that were often woven around various voyages and other important pieces of information. These stories were typically many generations old, and always repeated word for word. Any divergence from the prescribed version, even by as little as a word missed or out of sequence, would be harshly criticised. On an unforgiving ocean there was no margin for error, no matter how small.

For a young man to prove himself at this first hurdle, he would typically have to name the stars for the voyage to and from any number of islands, as well as the stars used in travelling from those islands to any other islands that might conceivably be visited. It was not good enough for a potential navigator to learn this knowledge by rote; in other words, in its prescribed place as part of a seemingly endless list. A navigator had to be able to make decisions immediately, and be able to reply with the exact information the moment his master asked him for the route between any two islands. This depth of knowledge and understanding has the benefit of preparing the navigator to be able to make fast, accurate decisions, even under stress.

After a young man had proven himself worthy of further instruction, his practical experience on the water could commence. First, he may have been introduced to the feel of the ocean swell by being laid on his back in

---

2. A more precise example highlights the difference between Carolinian and Marshallese navigation techniques in Micronesia. Because the Caroline archipelago is oriented east–west, the ocean swells that roll in are not interfered with to the same extent as those that strike the north–south oriented Marshall Islands. The Carolinians therefore rely on the unbroken roll of the swell to guide them during the voyages and birds to pinpoint land, while the Marshallese concentrate on reading wave interference patterns.

the ocean surrounding his home island. While floating, he could begin to appreciate the feel of different swells as they passed under him. He would also begin to become familiar with the seas around his own island. From this introductory stage, the successful student would progress through the various stages until he began putting his accumulated knowledge to the test on voyages with his master.

Once a young man had successfully graduated from the school for navigators, he could gather an experienced crew around him and commence testing himself on well-known routes to nearby islands or reefs.

On board the waka, the navigator usually claims the prime seating position. This is typically where the wind is able to strike his face without interference from the sails and where he is afforded a clear view of the ocean and the horizon ahead. His chosen spot was normally on the port side of the stern afterdeck (on the left side of the waka, towards the rear), as the sails commonly flow out to starboard (the right side).

While on these more routine voyages, the novice navigator would continue to hone his skills, particularly those required to estimate the waka's speed. To be sure of the exact position of the waka at any particular time, the navigator needed to be able to judge the distance he had travelled, and this required the ability to keep track of the ever-changing speed of his waka over many miles of open ocean sailing. The navigator's ability to achieve this challenging feat successfully was the accumulation of many years' experience, even from the time he first travelled in a waka as a child. The ability to judge speed, and therefore distance travelled, is absolutely crucial, and one of the major tests for a novice navigator.

A traditional navigator's job is universally acknowledged as having been extremely arduous. The need to keep awake for long periods of time was critical when using a system whereby the navigator relies on keeping a mental track of his vessel's progress.[3] This need to keep a constant vigil meant that he worked virtually non-stop during the voyage. To sleep for more than a few hours at a time could mean missing a vital sign, such as a critical star as it momentarily showed itself between clouds, or failing to detect a barely noticeable wind shift. It is said the navigator of a waka was easy to distinguish from his fellow crew members by his blood-shot eyes — no doubt testament to the strain of his job.

A voyage is divided into three main stages. First there is the departure and the setting of the primary course. This primary course takes into account any local sea or wind conditions likely to push the waka off course as it departs land. The second challenge for the navigator is to maintain the appropriate

3. It is recorded in some Polynesian traditions that a single waka would sometimes have two navigators assigned to it. This was possibly to lessen the strain on navigators during the longer voyages, for example to Hawaii or Aotearoa.

course en route, while the third objective is to reach the destination successfully.

While the basic sailing instructions taught to a navigator were designed to convey the general direction of his voyage, more complex information was needed to ensure a successful arrival. This included factors like the currents experienced when leaving an island and the names of alternative star paths to follow if necessary. Other information might include what sort of sea conditions to expect at various points along the way, or the course that could be sailed to nearby islands in case of emergency.

Departure

In the days before the commencement of a voyage, the navigator constantly goes over the probable star course. He also considers alternative routes, to be used should he encounter strong winds or ocean currents that might push him off the preferred course. After years of study and experience, the name and position of each star to be used during the night, and its position in relation to other stars as it rises or sets on the horizon, is already firmly set in his mind.

A departing waka aligning markers on land to help judge local currents.

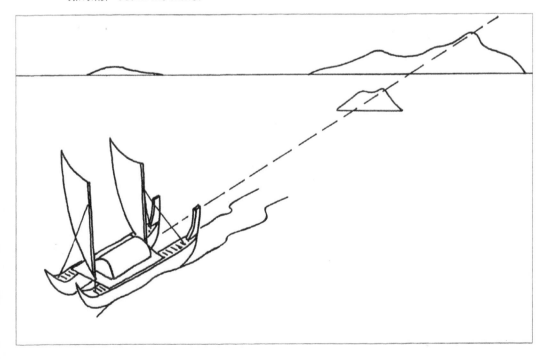

There appears to be no rule for the time of departure, but rather a set of customary times. For example, it might be preferable to depart at a certain hour to ensure a waka reaches the general area of the destination island at dawn, when the navigator can take advantage of birds flying out to their fishing grounds to pinpoint the position of the island (see the section on Birds below for an explanation). Other voyages might commence in the fading light so that backmarkers on shore can be used to establish the effect of any local currents before the stars become visible. Or the journey might start in the morning after fresh supplies have been gathered and food cooked. Family and friends then also have a chance to gather and farewell the crew before their daily routines begin. Having said their goodbyes, the crew board their waka and the voyage commences.

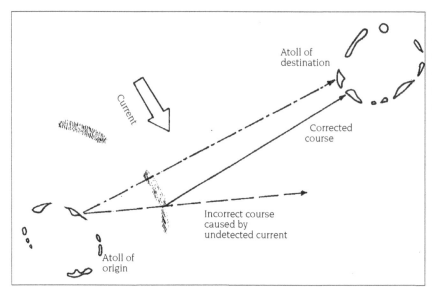

A crew sailing over a reef during a voyage is able check its progress and re-set the course if need be.

Most, if not all, important routes have a designated departure point, which is usually chosen so that two or more natural features can be easily lined up to act as a directional guide.

Features chosen include mountain and hill tops, trees, valleys and stars as they climb or set over a particular spot — in fact any features that can be lined up and relied upon to be in the same position year after year. Where no natural features are available, it is common to use man-made signs such as signal fires.

While the crew set about settling in for the voyage ahead, the navigator's work starts immediately. He has to carefully study the local current by watching for any sideways movement of the waka in relation to two chosen points on land and make allowance for any deviation from his course. From the outset there is no room for complacency.

Another aid to estimating current is to note the position of the waka as it sails over a known reef. Should any sideways current be encountered, it will force the waka off its primary course, and therefore over an unanticipated part of the reef. A vigilant navigator will observe this deviation and make the required adjustments.

Once clear of land, the navigator begins to familiarise himself with the roll of the ocean swell which is often used during daylight hours to stay on course, especially when the sky clouds over. To accomplish this, the navigator concentrates on the rhythm of the ocean as it lifts one end of the waka, then the other.

Having made himself familiar with the swell, the navigator is free to consciously search for any clues in his environment. By carefully studying the available aids such as the clouds, stars, sun and moon, or the many other signposts beneath and around him, he is able to piece together a mental picture of how his waka is progressing. It is just as important to know the exact position of the waka in relation to the island he has left, as it is to know the position of the intended destination at any time during the voyage. These two reference points are his principal life-lines, without which he can easily become hopelessly lost on the seemingly endless ocean. Often the navigator keeps the position of a third island in mind, to use in case of emergency. The real secret to a navigator's talent is his extraordinary skill in bringing together all of the pieces of information to ensure a successful voyage.

It is also the navigator's responsibility to take every possible safety precaution. It is not uncommon for a navigator to wait weeks or even months for the right wind conditions, or to sail on a roundabout course in order to take bearings from a well-known reef, or avoid an area of ocean that is considered dangerous.

Maintaining course

Once the voyaging waka has left the sanctuary of the inshore waters and the initial course is set, the navigator is faced with the responsibility of keeping the waka on course by mentally keeping track of its position. To achieve this, he is required to stay awake and alert for long periods at a time, if not for the entire voyage. To miss crucial signs that might alert him to a change in course could prove disastrous. His principal aids are the stars and sun, and the rolling swell of the ocean. Underwater reefs are also used.

Stars

Knowledge of the stars and their movement through the heavens is at the core of Polynesian navigational systems. The individual positions of the stars as they cut the horizon, either rising or setting, is the basis of the star compass. It is from these star-path points that the navigator takes his course bearings. Although the star compass consists of a fixed number of stars about the horizon, the navigator knows every star that follows the general path of these chosen stars through the heavens. It is almost as if the compass-point stars are the heads of their own star families. (The star compass should not be confused with the star path, which will be discussed later.)

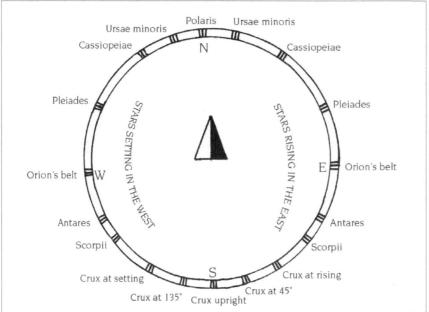

An example of a basic star compass. What makes a star compass work is that individual stars always rise from the same point in the east, and later set over corresponding point in the west. A navigator is therefore able to plot courses against the rising and setting point of stars with the knowledge that this course will stay the same, at least during his lifetime.

The stars that make up the star compass have been chosen through trial and error over many generations. An important factor in the choice of these particular stars is that they are well spaced in both time and direction. This is to ensure that there are at least one or two stars visible from the system at any hour of the night. By spreading the compass points about the sky there is also a reasonable chance that at least one well-known star will be visible should any part of the heavens cloud over. This allows the navigator to accurately judge the direction of all of the compass points in his system once he has a bearing on a familiar star.

When travelling on a clear night, the navigator is able to concentrate on his primary night-time navigational aid: the star path. A star path is a series of stars that either rise or set in the same part of the horizon. The stars of a star path are usually employed when they are still low in the sky, as it can be difficult to judge the exact spot that they have cut the horizon once they begin to climb high. Typically, ten to twelve stars are sufficient for a night's navigating, with the time each star is visible near the horizon well spaced throughout the night. It is common for the entire star path to be named after one of the more prominent stars featured within it, or, in some cases, by the name of the destination island.

Because very few stars actually cut the horizon in exactly the same spot as the preceding star, the navigator learns the necessary mental adjustments to be made as each star takes its turn as his guide. In learning a star path, the course may have been taught as 'a little to the left of star x, and then two fingers to the right of star y, straight at star z', and so on.

This use of the star-path sailing system needs to be adjusted somewhat for the voyage to Aotearoa. When sailing east–west or west–east through the Pacific, there are numerous stars setting or rising to guide the navigator. The night sky isn't so generous for the trip to Aotearoa, with few guiding stars setting in the south-west. A star path of sorts is still available, but the stars are concentrated more to the port side and behind the waka, rather than ahead.[4]

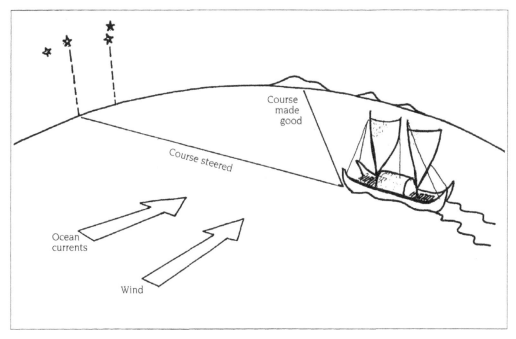

This diagram shows an example of the combined effect of wind and current on the course of a waka, highlighting the navigator's need to judge his environment accurately. If he fails to gauge either the wind or current strength correctly, he can easily miss his intended target.

Ocean swells

The use of ocean swells to help keep a waka on its course is quite common throughout the Pacific. Suitable swells are usually easily distinguishable from the locally produced waves, even within a few days of a major storm subsiding. Generally, localised waves are shorter and steeper, and have a breaking crest, while ocean swells are spaced wider apart and move across the ocean in a slow undulating motion. It is partly because of this regular rolling motion that navigators find it easier to feel a swell rather than watch it. When the night is clouded over, the navigator is often forced to rely on this regular ocean swell as his sole guide.

Should a navigator become totally disorientated during a cloudy night, he will usually lower his sail and wait until a star he recognises emerges from behind the clouds. His star knowledge is usually so great that he can figure out where his primary guiding star should be in relation to any other

4. See the chapter 'Talk of the navigators' for a list of the traditional guiding stars used during the voyage to Aotearoa.

known star that he may catch a glimpse of. He is then able to mentally re-align his waka with the help of the swell beneath him and confidently sail on with the knowledge that should he stray off course there will be an instant change to the roll of the waka. To achieve this level of skill, the navigator must learn the vast majority of stars that will be surrounding him on any voyage. Indeed, by the time he has graduated as a navigator he will have the entire night sky etched in his mind. On sighting virtually any star, he will be able to align it with one of his 'primary' stars, and thus adjust his course if necessary.

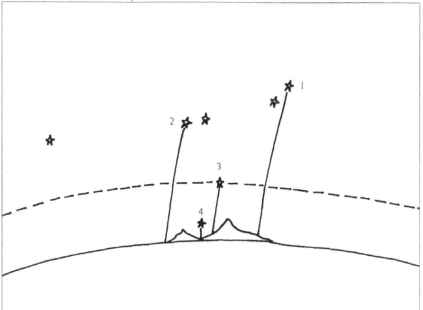

An example of a star path. In this example, the navigator would follow each star, 1 through 4, only changing stars as they reached an imaginary 'preferred height mark' (shown by the dotted line). He would use star 1 until it passed this mark, then star 2 until it too rose above the mark, and so on.

If, on the other hand, the sky is clouded over and there is a possibility that no stars will be visible at all, the navigator may have to rely on taking a fix for his course from the faintly visible sun before it sets. After years of training, the navigator knows the exact position of his chosen star path in relation to the setting sun and can mentally re-align the position of the star path with the point of sunset. Once this has been accomplished, the navigator can determine his course and re-acquaint himself with the roll of the swell, thus arming himself with a 24-hour-a-day reference.

A handy visual aid to back up the feel of the swell is to sight the exact spot the swell meets the hull of the waka. If the waka moves off course, the point of impact will correspondingly move along the hull.

The sun

The sun is another aid used to help keep a waka on course during a voyage. We have already seen how its position when setting on the horizon can be used when the sky is clouded over and the stars are likely to be obscured. It is interesting to note that while Matahi Brightwell was building the voyaging waka Hawaiki-nui, the sun's position in the sky for any time of the day and year became second nature to him. Without consciously studying it, Matahi had a 'feel' for where the sun should be in relation to the direction of his course.

A navigator is able to judge by the roll of the waka the direction the swell is coming from in relation to his course. If the roll of the waka changes, he knows the waka has strayed off course.

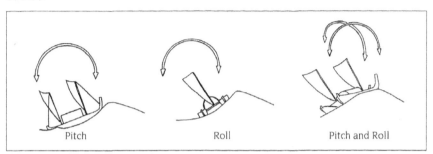

| Pitch | Roll | Pitch and Roll |

Other uses of the sun are not fully understood, but it is believed that the sun's rising position was aligned with the morning stars each dawn, as was its setting position with the evening stars at dusk. An experienced navigator was able to use this information along with the sun's ever-changing position during the day to assist him in his work.

Mid-ocean currents

The ability to read currents in mid-ocean and to be able to estimate the sideways drift of the waka are skills of great importance for any navigator. Without this knowledge, a waka can easily be pushed well off its course and miss its destination by many kilometres. While a large part of this skill can be put down to the navigator's experience and intuition, there are a few clues to be read from the ocean surface. The prime clues a navigator looks for are the shape and steepness of the waves, and the behaviour of the whitecaps.

The shape of each individual wave indicates both the direction and strength of a mid-ocean current. When the wave is travelling in the same direction as the wind, but the current is flowing against it, the wave appears steeper than usual. When the wind, current and wave are travelling in the same direction, the wave is smaller and flatter. If white caps appear to fold over gently and the froth disappears downwind in a long streak, the current is running with the wind. If, however, the whitecaps peak and are drawn back as they fall to windward (back towards the direction of the wind), the current is flowing against the wind.

Another clue, which is sometimes resorted to when the sea is calm or the waves too small to be of use, is the 'skin' of the water. If the current is flowing against the wind and wavelets, the water is said to look 'tight', and has barely detectable ripples running on the surface against the wind and wavelets. To be able to read the ocean surface to this degree competently takes years of intense study.

Reefs

The detection of known reefs is another method used to keep track of progress. In the clear unspoilt waters of the Pacific, reefs as deep as 30 fathoms (55 m) can be located by experienced navigators. A distinct change in the water's colour from blue to a light shade of green is often an indication of a reef deep below. An experienced man could even be relied upon to spot this change in colour during periods of rough weather.

Another way of detecting a reef in reasonably good weather is by looking for short, steep waves confined to a localised area. These waves are sometimes formed by underwater currents being forced up towards the surface when they meet an underwater obstruction such as a reef. These patches of rough water can be spotted from a good distance away if the surrounding water is flat.

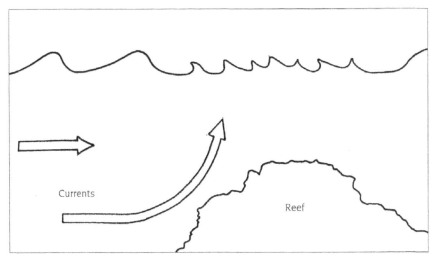

Currents

Reef

Isolated choppy areas of water in mid-ocean can sometimes be caused by underwater currents meeting a reef and being forced to the surface.

Finding land

Practical experience over the centuries has proven that the use of star paths and dead reckoning is not accurate enough in itself to ensure a successful voyage. Over time, Polynesian navigators recognised and studied a number of natural aids, resulting in very effective land-finding systems. This collection of techniques expands the target size of the island so that it is detectable well before it is actually visible. It is this expansion in size that determines the safety factor of any voyage, with a large target being substantially easier to detect.

If a number of these 'expanded' islands are spaced closely enough, their combined size forms what is sometimes referred to as an island block. By using all available clues, the navigator might end up searching for an island block some 240–320 km long, rather than an island of say 16 km.

By aiming for an island block, rather than a single island a few kilometres wide, the navigator can effectively increase the target size to the combined length of several islands, perhaps as much as 160 km or more.

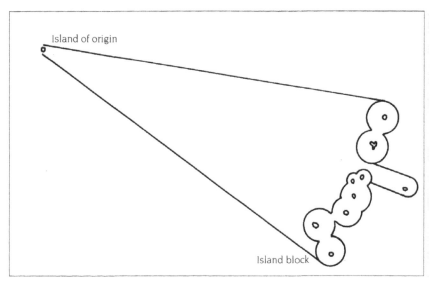

Waves

The use of swell patterns to indicate the presence of land is believed to have been widespread in the Pacific, with the only factor limiting its effectiveness being the underwater size of the island or atoll being sought. As with the use of swells in navigating in the open ocean, it is the feel of the swell rather than any visual clue that alerts the navigator.

When searching for land, one of the techniques employed by a navigator is to try to detect any change to the regular swell. He knows that should there be any change in the pattern, it is usually because a swell has met with an island or atoll and been bent around it. At the point where the two ends of the

Swell refraction patterns are caused by waves bending around islands. An experienced navigator can pick such changes in most weather conditions.

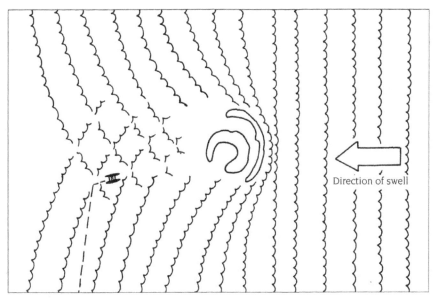

Direction of swell

'bent' swell meet on the lee side of the island, a choppy area of sea is created. By recognising this change to the feel of the ocean, caused by the swell's refraction, and reading the clues available to him from the size and angle of these localised waves, it is possible for an experienced navigator to detect the presence of a land mass and its direction long before it is visible.

Another clue is the reflection of a swell after it bounces off an island. This change is obvious to an experienced navigator from any angle, but particularly so from dead ahead. When sailing straight towards an island with the swell coming from behind, the waka is swept forward by the main swell, before the navigator feels a slight hesitancy as his vessel is slowed by the slapping of reflected waves meeting the hull. This reflection is relatively easy to detect, as not only is the swell shorter in length than the main swell, but it is flowing on an angle at odds with the main swell. Once located, the navigator has only to turn directly into the reflected swell to ensure he finds land. It is reported that this phenomenon can be detected as far as 56 km out at sea in ideal conditions. It is also regarded as a particularly useful land-finding tool in overcast weather.

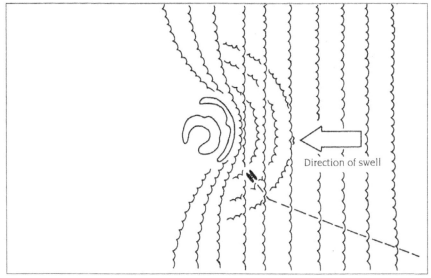

Direction of swell

Swell reflection is caused by waves bouncing back off islands along their original path. They too are used as a guide to finding land.

Birds

It is well known among Polynesian navigators that certain birds can be relied upon at dawn and dusk to indicate the direction of land. All of these birds sleep on land at night, and are guaranteed to fly in a direct line from land to their feeding grounds in the mornings and return directly back to land in the evenings. It is this consistency and reliability that is of significance to a navigator.

The most common birds that a navigator relies on are boobies, terns and noddies. Each of these can be relied upon to stay within 40 to 48 km of land during their search for food. Navigators are not so much interested in how far out from an island they can come across individual birds, but in how far out the birds can reliably be seen in groups. This is because larger groups of birds are generally considered a more reliable indication that land is nearby than individual birds.

With this understanding, the navigator can confidently estimate how far from land he is when he encounters land birds at sea. If there are few birds, he can suppose land to be from 32 to 40 km off. If there are many birds feeding, he can safely guess the waka to be between 16 and 32 km from land. If it is less than 16 km, the crew would be able to spot the island directly, while if they were more than 32 km out, the number of birds would be substantially less.

The navigator will, of course, have to wait until evening when the birds fly straight back home before he can confirm the direction of land. At that time it will usually be too dangerous to sail on blindly in the steadily darkening evening if he is approaching an unfamiliar island or atoll. Instead, the waka might be cautiously sailed a short distance in the direction the birds took, with the knowledge that land must be in excess of 16 km away (otherwise the crew would have seen it themselves). The sail is then taken down and the crew anxiously await first light, ever hopeful that the current doesn't push them so far from land that the birds aren't visible flying out in the morning to their fishing grounds.

If a navigator becomes lost, or is unsure of the exact position of an island, the sight of land-based birds feeding in groups is of immense comfort to him.

Clouds

Clouds, so often visible over islands, are a helpful sign to navigators as they search for land. They provide a number of clues, but it is their movement as they form over islands and break away downwind that is the most important sign. Moving freely as they approach an island, the clouds seem to slow down as they draw near to the land mass, while to leeward (downwind) small clouds continually break off and speed away with the wind. When searching for land, the navigator looks for these clouds continuously reforming over the same spot, hour after hour. Clouds seen acting like this are considered a sure sign of land below.

Another clue provided by clouds is a V-shaped cloud formation that is sometimes seen above islands. This is most obvious when the weather is calm and there are few clouds in the sky. The centre of a stationary cloud is pulled down towards the land, forming the V-shape. The phenomenon is sometimes also noticeable in cloudy, windy weather. In these circumstances the V-shaped cloud sits in the one position above an island, while other clouds continually blow in and join it before departing in broken formation downwind.

The reflection of land colour on the underside of the cloud is also used to locate land. Wet coral reefs and coral sand give a whitish reflection, while islands with vegetation produce a dark reflection. Atolls and islands with large dry reefs often reflect a pinkish tinge. These reflected colours are usually very subtly different to the colours of other clouds in the general vicinity that are not situated directly over the island.

As with most of the techniques employed to locate land, studying clouds takes perseverance. A navigator will typically study the horizon for hours before he can be sure that a particular cloud bank signifies land.

Phosphorescence

Visible anywhere between 16 and 160 km from shore, phosphorescence appears as flashes and streaks of light originating from the direction of land. Known as Te Lapa and Te Mata in different parts of the Pacific, this phenomenon is reportedly easiest to see between 50 and 130 km from land, and is observed anywhere from 45 cm to over 1.8 m under the surface.

One authority states that the longer flashes travel from the land, while the shorter flashes travel back towards it. Phosphorescence moves in one direction or the other in turn, rather than shooting backwards and forwards at the same time, and the closer to land the sighting is, the faster the movement of the flashes. It is an especially useful tool for navigators to use on overcast nights when stars are clouded over. Although it is still unclear exactly what Te Lapa is and how it is created, one suggestion is that it is related to the motion of reflected waves returning after bouncing off islands.

A rare reference to phosphorescence in Maori tradition is recorded in *The Peopling of the North*. It reads:

> To the east of Whangaroa there is a projecting point where the water is very clear; it is called Te Au-kanapana, or flashing current; and it is here that Kupe is said to have made land on his voyage from Hawaiki. It is one of the places also where canoes used to take their departure from in going back to Hawaiki.[5]

In another version this 'flashing current' is called Te Au Kanapanapa.

A further observation that is possibly connected to the explanation of this phenomenon comes from the navigator Abera of Nikunau, who stated that:

> ... on calm, cloudless days, when the sun was nearly overhead, this sign was to be looked for: you peered down into the sea and observed the sun's rays. Some rays would be long and some short. The shorter rays pointed toward the invisible land.[6]

5. S. Percy Smith, *The Peopling of the North*: 15.
6. David Lewis, *We the Navigators*: 211.

Drift objects, seaweed and sea life

Although the presence of drift objects is not of much use in working out how far from land a waka may be, it can help in determining which direction the land is if the currents can be discerned. Another pointer is the long lines of seaweed that can sometimes be encountered at sea. Lines of seaweed have been recorded extending up to 200 km from the coast of Aotearoa eastward into the Pacific. This seaweed is progressively more widespread the closer one gets to the coast. Sea life also becomes far more prolific, with sharks and dolphins frequently seen on the surface.

Zenith stars

The zenith star method of finding land relies on the navigator deliberately sailing to either the west or east of an island, and then confirming his latitude (north–south position on the globe) by positioning his waka immediately beneath the path of a star that is known to pass directly over the targeted island. The navigator then has the relatively easy task of sailing along the star's longitude (east–west path) in the direction of his destination.

There are suggestions for zenith star systems from Tonga, Tahiti and Tikopia in David Lewis's *We the Navigators*. Some of Lewis's examples leave room for misinterpretation, and modern-day navigators of the standing of Nainoa Thompson and Mau Piailug find the zenith star system of no practical use. Mau goes as far as saying that it is 'just playing around' and that it 'has no meaning' for him.

Reading the weather

The ability to read and forecast the weather is also an important skill for a navigator to develop. Much time and effort is expended in studying the natural signs in the days leading up to a voyage. There are many clues, among the more obvious being the shape and colour of the cloud formations. Over the generations a navigator's predecessors learnt how to read these clouds, and what the variations meant. Most of the following examples are from Micronesia, and are used to illustrate the variety of weather indicators available to navigators in the Pacific.

Small cirrus clouds seen near the sun at dawn indicate that any existing breeze will continue, but the same type of cloud seen at night suggests that the strength of the wind will increase significantly. A large bank of stratus clouds to the south might indicate that stormy weather is due in the next few days, while a black cloud will usually signify rain and a little wind, and a cloud with a brown tinge suggests strong winds.

Another sign available to weather forecasters on land is the behaviour of ants as they go about their daily routines. The sight of large numbers of ants returning to their nests with food is frequently a sign of impending bad weather. Should they block the entrance holes to their nest, storms are almost guaranteed.

Similarly, the behaviour of certain types of crab is also a clue to the coming weather. Should the entrance to the crab's hole be blocked and the surrounding sand flattened, rain and wind is due within the next few days. If the entrance is open, but the surrounding sand flattened, there will be no rain but plenty of wind. A blocked hole without the sand having been flattened signals rain and no wind. Finally, an unblocked hole and heaped sand foretells fine weather and little or no wind. It is important in this instance, however, for the navigator to study crabs that dig their entrance holes straight down to be assured of an accurate forecast.

Birds are also a favoured signal of expected foul weather: in Rarotonga, frigate birds returning to shore unexpectedly is a reliable sign of impending bad weather.

Survival skills

It is recorded in a small number of accounts that the ancient Polynesians knew of a herb or plant that when chewed would allow them in cases of emergency to drink seawater without the usual effects. Another account, this one from modern times, tells of a navigator from Butaritari who accustomed his body to the effects of drinking seawater during the seven years of his navigation training. It is claimed that if necessary he could go without fresh water for weeks at a time.

Other skills known to have been adopted by various Polynesians included the Hawaiian practice of throwing kukui-nut oil into the waters surrounding the waka when a storm was approaching. The oil is said to have had the same effect that modern-day oil spillages have in calming the ocean surface.

The crew of Tahiti-nui used this technique during their voyage to Chile in 1956. In danger of being swamped by a huge following sea, they stuffed a T-shirt full of cotton wool, soaked it in cooking oil, then, having screwed it up into a ball, threw it from their stern tied to a rope. As soon as the small oil slick formed, the waves actually parted to either side of the raft, averting a near certain disaster.

The men of Santa Cruz have been known purposely to swamp their waka in an effort to limit damage from incoming storms, while the use of the conch shell to get the attention of other waka was known throughout the Pacific.

PART TWO

IN THE WAKE OF KUPE

INTRODUCTION TO PART TWO

Perhaps more than 800 years after the last voyaging canoe reached Aotearoa, Greg Whakataka-Brightwell relived the trials and hardships of his ancestors during the epic voyage of the Polynesian waka Hawaiki-nui in 1985. With little more than a dream and incredible determination, Matahi, as he was later named by the Tahitians, hand built the 22-m voyaging waka, and along with a crew of four, led by his father-in-law Francis Cowan, sailed her from Tahiti to Aotearoa using traditional Polynesian navigation techniques. The crew were also without the luxury and support of an escort boat during the entire voyage.

This is the story of Hawaiki-nui.

The following chapters are based on interviews conducted in January and April 1998. Meetings were held at both Matahi's Gisborne home and Whangara, the worksite of his latest project, the 45-m waka taua Nukutaimemeha.

GETTING STARTED

Realising a dream

Hawaiki-nui actually means more to me than a lot of people think. People think I just built it and sailed it for the reputation of helping the Maori culture, and to a certain extent that is true. But I also built it to bring the ocean and canoe culture back to our people. I also built it to help my ancestors. I did it for a number of reasons.

There was a strong spiritual influence that drove me to complete Hawaiki-nui. After I lost my grandmother I began to have a recurring vision. We say the Maori spirit always goes back to Hawaiki-nui. In the dream I saw that the spiritual road of my ancestors was broken, and that the only way to repair it so that my ancestors could go back to Hawaiki was to sail the canoe. In my dream, my grandmother and all my ancestors were on this mountain, and they could not find the path leading to Hawaiki. I could not see all of their faces, just my grandmother's, and she was saying to me, 'Hurry up. We can't get off the mountain. We can't find the path back to Hawaiki. We need the path, and you need to sail the canoe to repair the path so that we can be free to go back to Hawaiki.'

I had that dream every couple of nights during the whole time I was building Hawaiki-nui. The dream seemed so real. Some nights during the actual voyage I could see a crowd of people following us, the spirits of my ancestors — it was beautiful, not threatening at all. They were on the path and they could see it had been repaired, it was not broken any longer. But in my heart I would think, 'What have I done wrong? Have I messed up the path for my grandmother and all my relatives to go back to Hawaiki?' I was really worried that I would do something wrong to affect them.

After the voyage, that particular dream of my grandmother and ancestors stopped. When we arrived in Hicks Bay it was the first thing I thought that night: I was afraid I would go to sleep and my grandmother would pop up and say, 'Hey you, there's no path yet!' But it never came back.

To me, it is one of the main things in my life to have renewed that spiritual road of my ancestors with the canoe. For me that link between our Maori heaven and the physical world became a reality with Hawaiki-nui.

There are other sides too. Through my wife, Raipoia, we physically reunited Tahiti, Ra'iatea, Rarotonga and Aotearoa. Raipoia's mother is Tahitian and her father, the navigator Francis Cowan, is from Ra'iatea and Rarotonga. When we arrived in Rarotonga, the Rarotongans understood the significance of the voyage straight away — not so much the canoe, but the physical reuniting of the islands. The island of Tahiti, the island of Ra'iatea, the island of Rarotonga, and now Aotearoa. The Rarotongans told us that through our children we had linked all the traditions together.

Matahi Brightwell at Whangara beside his latest project, the 45-m waka taua Nukutaimemeha

I guess the desire has always been in the hearts of our great teachers to build a voyaging canoe. For me, the inspiration came from my mentors, Rua Kaika and Kohe Webster, who were the initial driving force behind it all. They planted the seeds in my mind while we were carving my tribal meeting house, Toa Rangatira in Porirua. The idea for the project came from these two, handed down to me as the apprentice to fulfil it. Even with their support, it took from 1974 to 1978 to find enough backing for the idea and the right trees before we could start.

The main delay to starting the project was a total lack of support from Maori. I have never spoken about it before, but I spent eleven years learning my traditional skills, and when I finished my apprenticeship and was ready to start building Hawaiki-nui, most of my elders told me that I should forget my dreams and get a real job. I could not accept that, so I turned to the mana and authority held within our own direct family. I turned to my grandmother, Te Huatahi Gilbert, who sent me to her cousin Matenga Baker, who in turn directed me to my elders John Gardiner and Kohe Webster. John and Kohe were then able to advise me about what traditional canoe-building knowledge was left in our iwi.

Other direct support came from my grand-uncle Heta Gilbert, who taught me genealogy for three years during my carving training, and his brother Arohanui, who gave me plenty of good advice. It was Arohanui who said to me, 'The one way that you will achieve this is by naming the two hulls after your great-grandparents, Whareahuru Gilbert and Purewa Tahiwi,' which I did after getting family permission. Without his wisdom I don't think I could have done it.

After the family agreed to the names for the hulls, Arohanui took me aside for another talk. 'These two hulls are going to be named after your ancestors, don't ever abandon them.' The wisdom behind that little talk showed a lot of foresight. The decision to name the hulls after my ancestors really kept me going during the many low times I had. I mean, how could I even consider abandoning my own ancestors?

Arohanui continued to support me all along. People were complaining to him about the way I dressed, my hair was too long, I wouldn't socialise, I was arrogant. Of course that was all true, but I had to be that way to achieve my goal. They bred that into me. My elders brought me up to learn the Maori side of my life and instilled those strengths in me. Yes, I'm arrogant, because I believe in myself. All those qualities came from my elders.

The trees

During the weeks leading up to the selection of the trees, Rua Kaika taught me everything he knew about selecting totara. But it was all by word of mouth. We didn't have a chance to go into the Whirinaki State Forest, where we'd been granted permission to source our wood. Another big challenge! When selecting totara, the main thing to look at is the bark. Rua told me not to select a tree with spongy bark, because that meant there would be too much sapwood and the grain wouldn't be strong enough for a canoe. He also told me to avoid trees standing on the snowline or on the side of a hill. Trees close to the valley floor are better nourished and have stronger grain. I also had to find trees with strong, thick bark: thin bark suggests that the tree is still maturing, and therefore the grain will be too loose.

The other way of checking the health of trees is to scrape the undergrowth away from the roots, and look for the tap-root system. It's like the heart of the tree, and I had to see if it was rotten. If the roots were suffering from decay, I wasn't to take the tree out. I was only allowed two trees. If I chose one tree and we felled it, and it was rotten inside, then I was not allowed the second one. I needed two healthy trees for the project, so I was under a lot of pressure.

It took about ten days before I found the trees I wanted. The ranger,

Bob Collins, took me to trees he thought I might want, and each time I'd go through my routine. First I'd look up top. Rua told me that if there are broken branches and kiekie growing from the top, then rain has seeped down through the grain and ruined the tree. That's how you get dry rot. The ranger was looking at me doing all my stuff, and he asked, 'What are you doing?' I replied, 'I'm just doing what I'm told!' He walked away shaking his head.

Finally, after looking at literally hundreds of trees, we came across the ones I wanted. We were walking down towards a flat area, and I noticed these two trees growing not far from each other, about 12 m apart. The colour of the bark was orange-grey. I said to the ranger, 'Those are the ones. I can see the canoes inside them. They're the canoes I want!'

The ranger looked at me kind of funny and said, 'They're not canoes, they're trees.'

'Well they look like canoes to me.' And that's how I found them.

When it came to milling the trees, we had a bit of an argument on our hands. I don't know who decided it, but someone had told the ranger that I was to get the trees there and then. It was mid-December and the trees were full of sap. He told me, 'You take them now or you're not getting them.' The best time for cutting totara is between mid-June and early July, when the sap is at its lowest, and the trees are at their lightest.

The ceremony prior to cutting down the two totara trees in Whirinaki State Forest involved both traditional and Ratana prayer side by side.

I didn't know what to do, so I went and saw Rua and told him the problem. We knew the trees were going to be twice as heavy compared to a June cutting, but we had no choice. We had to take them in December. Another thing was that I knew Rua was getting old, so I made the decision to take them. So about a month later we cut them. That added a full two years to the project, because I had to wait for the trees to cure properly.

Volunteers working in the purpose-built workshed at Haamoa marae, Pahiatua. Wood chips are piled up outside the shed, waiting to be burned.

When the time came to cut down the trees, we asked the Ratana minister from Pahiatua and the elder and chairman of the Ikaroa District Council, John Tangiora, to do a joint ceremony — traditional Maori and Ratana church side by side. A lot of people joined in the ceremony. After the ceremony and karakia were completed, two New Zealand representative axemen cut the trees down with a double-handled saw. We had originally hoped to use traditional adzes, but because we had to take the trees six months earlier than anticipated, we didn't have time to make them. All the same, we were determined not to use power tools.

During the ceremony and before the cutting started, the forest was full of bird song. Then, as soon as we started to cut the scarf the birds quietened. There was a little bit of noise about during the scarf cutting, but as soon as the first tree hit the forest floor there was complete silence. It was an eerie feeling, being in that huge forest and no noise about us — just silence. I don't think that the enormity of the project really dawned on me until that moment. I had actually to prove physically that Maori traditional knowledge is still intact and can still be applied today. Immediately I thought, 'What the hell have I done?'

Fortunately for me, the trees proved to be the perfect choice. So we were all there with high expectation. The next thing I knew Tim Shadbolt started to cry. I think the moment got to him, and that got me started! It was a very emotional moment for everyone there. Then Dun Mihaka called in a big voice, 'Hey you two, tears are not going to get this canoe finished.' That sort of snapped us into action, and we prepared to move the trees.

The trees were only about five minutes from the road, and with the help of the Whirinaki State Forest administration we managed to move them to our waiting truck. First stop was Taupo, then on to Tuwharetoa where I have whanau. There we had a ceremony to bless the trees and the project, with Sir Hepi Te Heuheu's son Timmy. From there we went down to Hawke's Bay, and Pahiatua.

The whole community of Pahiatua got in behind the project, which was based at the local marae, Haamoa. Matenga Baker came over for the blessing of the actual worksite. My elders, Uncle Heta and Uncle Nui, were too old to travel by then, and Rua was too sick and couldn't come either. But Kohe was able to attend, and Tuhoe representing my mother's side came to support me as well.

When it came to advice concerning canoe construction, my main sources of knowledge were Rua Kaika and John Taiapa. There was an agreement between Rua and John, who was then the head carver at the Rotorua Institute of Carving. Rua would send me there about once every two months for a couple of days and John would give me advice and a historical perspective on Maori art. At the same time Rua concentrated on the physical side, the technique. Without this additional help I don't think I could have ever achieved my dream.

John also passed on a couple of useful tricks of the trade to me. After his 30 or 40 years of art projects for Maori, his words of advice to me were well proven, and I treated them like treasures. 'When you build this canoe, you cut all the wood and you spread it all around the workshop to make it look like the project is nearly finished. So when your critics come past, or come to see you, they'll think there's a lot of work going on, but what you're really doing is still working on the hulls.'

So that's what I did. Every second week during the time we were working on the hulls, I'd change the workshop's appearance. That meant moving a lot of timber about, and shifting the big beams from one end to the other — making it look like the canoe was getting near completion. John also advised me not to discuss the project too deeply with tribal members because it might lead to problems with misuse of information. I followed his advice without reservation.

Rua, Kohe and John Gardiner also forbade me to read books. They didn't want the world to claim that I got the information out of books. Likewise, I didn't draw a plan of the canoe on paper. Instead, I had dreams. During some of the early television interviews they asked me, 'How do you work it out without a drawn plan?' I told them straight: 'I sleep, and I have a dream. It's like I'm watching a big cinema screen, and I see what I'm going to do the next day. When I go to work the next day, that's what I do.' I'm sure everyone thought I was mad!

Once in Pahiatua, the first problem I had to tackle was to study the trees and decide which side would form the belly of each hull. Because the trees were so heavy with sap when we cut them, they received splits — big splits — along their sides when they hit the forest floor. So it took me about three weeks to study them, with the help of timberjacks, before I even started.

Of course everyone was on my back to get started. But I always stuck to John Taiapa's advice: 'Don't worry about people saying start now, start now. Take the bark off and check the trees. Take your time!' We had to turn the tree so that the splits would be on the side to be hollowed out, reducing the chances of weak timber affecting the sides and belly of the hulls. Traditional sailing canoes had heavy keel construction, so the belly had to be particularly strong and very thick. We kept the thickness of Hawaiki-nui's belly to about 600 mm. The thickness helps with both stability in the water and the overall strength of the canoe. In the end we had to work around the cracks, and in fact had to go as far as partially redesigning the hulls.

Talking about the hull design, one thing Maori should be educated in is that our canoes weren't designed to be anchored in the harbour. We ran our canoes onto the beach, and the hull has to be constructed to allow for this.

When you are carving totara, shaping it every day, you begin to understand the properties, the inner qualities of the wood. You become so sensitive to the wood you can almost feel it breathing, sweating. Totara sweats. There's a resin inside that comes out of the pores of the wood, and if you leave it for two or three weeks, well, you can see that resin coming out. And that's what Hawaiki-nui gave me. It gave me the opportunity to have a deeper insight into the wood. There are perhaps thirteen different grain colours, ranging from yellow-brown to purple-red, and some have flecks of orange in them. Each colour signifies a different stage in its cycle. Totara trees function very similarly to people. So now when I go into the bush, I understand the nature of the tree. When it comes to building a waka — or anything, for that matter — if someone looking at the form doesn't understand the depth of the work and thought gone into the construction, then they can't really appreciate it.

For example, when we were fitting a gunnel butt-join to a rib, we'd have to consider the number of pegs needed to hold that gunnel in place and the spacing of those pegs. Then we had to work out where the lashing holes were going to be placed between the pegs, and the individual size for that particular lashing hole. You've got to calculate everything precisely, because every part of the construction has to do with survival and success. It drives you to do things properly. But if you don't understand the depth of the grain of the wood you're working with, then you can't predict how the wood is going to react under pressure. If you don't understand the nature of the material you're working with, you can't shape the wood to its maximum and you can't use it to its maximum.

Once we got started on the hulls, I found that my main problem was that I was the only one who knew about shaping out totara hulls with adzes. So I had to teach my helpers. I taught them by setting up a string-line the length of the log, and then showed them how to adze between the string-line and the log. This helped them to get a straight line and not to cut too deep. I usually had to go over their work because I am really particular. But what they actually helped me do was the main shaping, while I did the finishing, using those vertical concave channels that run the length of the bottom of the hull. The channels create an air-bubble cushion for the canoe to ride on, and it's true — I've seen it happen. There is less resistance on the hull, and it also assists the steering under pressure. The channels are called ngatoa in Maori.

It took eight months of adzing to complete the hulls. During most of that time I was under heavy criticism for taking too long on them. The adzing actually took eight months of hard, hard adzing, every day. At that stage, I was mainly using the shipwright's adze, carving chisels, and the odd chainsaw for squaring off big blocks of wood. When it came to the real work of shaping the hulls, we used only hand tools.

The labour of volunteers was a major help in carving the mid-gunnels and shaping the hulls of Hawaiki-nui.

One request I had from my teachers was to burn all the woodchips and off-cuts from the project. In Pahiatua we probably had something like 4 tonnes of chips, and we had the fire going every day. Then we spread the ash over the worksite. The only timber we let go off-site were the heart sections of the two trees. We had decided before we even started the adzing to offer them to the iwi in gratitude for supporting the project. One went to Woodville and the other to Pahiatua. Also during the adzing of the hulls I got a call from John Paki, a relation of mine who was renovating a famous temple called Te Miringa Te Kakara. He wanted our bark for the church, but I had to refuse. I felt sorry, but I had to stand on the advice of my teachers. No parts other than the heart sections were to go anywhere else because it was such a sacred canoe.

So, in the end, the majority of the adze work on the hull was done in Pahiatua, with a bit done at Porirua and some light finishing when we later moved the project to Tahiti. That's where we set the bow and stern. We had to set the stern and bow covers first, then finish off the adzing to marry the bow shape to the bow cover. That's the only adzing we did in Tahiti.

A chance encounter: Francis Cowan

Francis Cowan happened to be in Dunedin, having brought a very close friend of his from Ra'iatea for treatment at the hospital. Francis had dreamed of building a voyaging canoe ever since 1956, when he was on the Tahiti-nui for the voyage from Tahiti to Chile. He had actually started to build a canoe in the mid-1960s, but lost it in a fire in 1967 before it had been completed. In the intervening years he had been searching for replacement trees within French Polynesia, but had failed to locate any that were suitable. Anyway, while he was passing time in his motel unit he happened to see a documentary on the TV programme *Te Koha* about me building the canoe. Francis immediately rang his mate Greig (Ace) Cuthers in Auckland, and asked him to track me down.

Ace went to Hoani Waititi marae to try to get my contact number, and to speak to someone about me. Apparently they weren't very complimentary about me, even though we had never met! Nevertheless, Francis wanted to meet me and wrote me a letter introducing himself. In the letter he said he had always dreamt that he would one day build a canoe, ever since he had been on Tahiti-nui. He finished his introduction by explaining that he was a descendant of the last king of Bora Bora. I was quite taken aback and didn't know what to do. In the end I went and saw my elders Arohanui Gilbert, Uncle Heta and Rua Kaika. They read the letter, and Rua said to me, 'Well, his dream's older than ours. He has the right bloodlines, so we've got to give the canoe to him.'

By this time, Francis had already returned to Tahiti, so I had to ring him and try to arrange a meeting. I was dead broke, so Francis agreed to fly back from Tahiti for a meeting at Ace's Auckland home. It was July 1980 by this time. In fact, I was so broke that even after a whip around between the guys working on Hawaiki-nui at that time, there was only enough money to pay for my train fare one way. I rang my mate Tim Shadbolt in Auckland and asked him to meet me at the railway station and take me to the meeting. As arranged, Tim met me at the railway station, arriving on time in his old beat-up truck. There was a big hole in the back window, and by the time we arrived at Ace's place we were covered with cement dust and we stank of concrete. I don't think Ace's first impression of me was too great!

Once the meeting started, and I'd had a chance to sit back and listen to Francis, I sensed that this project was bigger than I thought. Francis himself was one of the last traditional canoe builders of Tahiti. He and his friend Tutaha Salmon had built the fleet of canoes for the Marlon Brando film *Mutiny on the Bounty*, using traditional techniques, and the knowledge that I lacked — the art of lashing, and the rigging used for traditional sail — was second nature to him. He knew about all of that, so I was really excited. After the meeting Francis invited me to visit him in Tahiti to look things over. While I was over there he took me to the sacred marae of Taputapuatea. I was really very impressed with Francis and his set-up.

When I came home I told my elders what I had heard and seen. After a week of discussion my elders decided that we were giving him the canoe. The change in plans meant we wouldn't be sailing from Aotearoa to Tahiti, but from Tahiti to Aotearoa. We were going to do it from our spiritual origin back to Aotearoa. We were renewing the spiritual path from Ra'iatea to Aotearoa. It made sense to me. So all those things sort of fitted into place.

I rang Francis up to tell him we were giving him the canoe, but that there was one condition. I insisted that he come to New Zealand to meet with the elders of my family. He readily agreed, and I organised a meeting with Matenga Baker, Rua Kaika, Kohe Webster and several others of my immediate family. When it came time for the meeting, my grand-uncle Arohanui Gilbert asked Francis straight to his face, 'And who are you that we should give you my parents? You realise these two hulls are named after my parents? And my grand-nephew — we're giving him to you as well.'

Francis calmly replied that he was from Ra'iatea, Tahaa and Rarotonga, and said that if he was given the canoe he promised to help us realise the dream of sailing from Tahiti to Aotearoa.

My grand-uncle continued: 'You realise our hapu holds the church Rangiatea, and strangely, you come from Ra'iatea. I believe that this coming together has happened because the Maori won't help my grand-nephew. It looks like the circumstances in the universe are bringing these things to happen because there's too much opposition here. He probably won't even do it because the opposition's so strong against him. It is the best way.'

And it was the best way. In the mid- to late 1970s it wasn't trendy to be Maori, and if you were obviously pushing something that was Maori, it was immediately going to be restricted. Again the wisdom of my grand-uncle prevailed.

At that stage the project was beginning to come together beyond my will and my power. It came together because no one here in Aotearoa would lift a finger. It seemed to me like all the powers of the universe were involved, and making improbable connections. How did I know Francis was going to be here bringing a sick friend soon after I had a rare television interview? How did I know he was going to switch the TV on and there I would be

Rua Kaika's students at Maraeroa carving whakapapa (genealogies) on the mid-gunnels.

building the canoe of his dreams? How did I know, and how did he know, that my origin in Otaki is linked to Rangiatea church?

I still didn't know what my elders had in mind for me, until Matenga's speech. He said, 'Take this canoe from us, the tribe of Raukawa, because this boy is going to be stamped on. You're not only saving the canoe, you're saving us, you're saving him. So take him.' And they pointed to me. 'And you go with the canoe.' I looked at him, all the while thinking, 'Okay, if you say so!' Yeah, that was a fascinating time.

We shut the project down in Pahiatua as soon as the canoe was formally handed over to Francis. It was March 1981, and when I look at it now the handover came at the right time. Around that time I was embroiled in a dispute over the misuse of project funds. It took a lot of effort to convince the community that I was not involved in the misappropriation of funds, and that the blame lay with others not involved in the project proper. I had to call on the help of all my friends, like Vince Burke and the late Jim Booth. The dispute took a lot out of me, it really drained me.

So despite the community's initial assistance and backing, I was actually glad to leave Pahiatua. Rua had started a carving school at Maraeroa in Porirua, and I had to take over the day-to-day instruction because he was too sick. He was old and quickly losing his strength. Rua had also asked for the canoe to be near his workshop so he could see the work being done on the hulls.

The only other work we did in Aotearoa was to carve the genealogy of my two great-grandparents on the mid-gunnels for the canoe. That took about six months with help from Rua's students. That's the only work we did in Porirua. The rest, like the rigging, the decks and the crossbeam fittings, was done in Tahiti. All the wood for that came from Francis.

THE MOVE TO TAHITI

When the time came to move the project to Tahiti, the hulls were 90 percent finished and the gunnels were complete. A friend of my father organised the building of a cradle for the hulls, and then we transported them up to Orakei marae in Auckland. There we had to wait two weeks for our ship, the *Bounty*, to arrive, and then it was off to Tahiti. When we arrived, word came through that Rua had passed on. That was a particularly hard time for me.

The two hulls, Whareahuru and Purewa, at Maraeroa in Porirua, awaiting transport to Auckland and on to Tahiti.

After all the problems and setbacks in Aotearoa, and Rua's passing, I was looking for a fresh, trouble-free start in Tahiti, but things weren't to be that easy. Pengally's Transport in Aotearoa had to have a price for the canoe for insurance purposes, so it was valued at US$100,000. Unfortunately, Tahitian customs latched on to that fact and when we arrived in Tahiti we had to pay a 10 percent tax levy. Francis had to find US$10,000 to get the canoe out of customs, and that took nearly two and a half months. While he was trying to find the money, the canoe was sitting in the open on the wharf. Fortunately, the hulls didn't seem to be affected by the hot, humid conditions.

In the end, Francis's half-brother, Gerard, brokered a deal with the government for us. He was employed by the Office Territorial D'Action Culturelle (OTAC), the cultural centre in Tahiti. The government agreed to help with the funding, to arrange payment of the US$10,000, but we had to hand the ownership of the project over to OTAC. They were to manage the finance and the administration of the canoe while we built it. That's how the French Polynesian government got involved, and how the canoe building turned into a Tahitian project.

So there I was in Tahiti. Imagine me, in my very early twenties, just a boy, and here I arrive in Tahiti with Francis. It was a real cultural awakening for me. I went from a culture that was at that time quickly losing its language, into one that had never lost its language. I was going into a culture that gave me a better insight into my own history. I owe a lot of the success of Hawaiki-nui, as well as my own success, to the Tahitians.

Another highlight for me was that Tahiti is canoe heaven. Every second householder is a canoe builder and every second house has a fishing or racing canoe sitting outside. But even with their rich and living canoe culture, I can tell you our project created quite a stir.

Because Francis and I had to rely on government funding, they had insisted on bringing in canoe experts. We had quite a few confrontations over what was the best hull shape. I told them, 'This is the shape and I'm not changing.' Most of their knowledge was for flat-water racing, not ocean-going voyages. I told them that the hulls were going to be this shape because of my dream. Francis pulled me aside and said something like, 'You can't actually say that: that it's going to be like such and such because of your dream!' I didn't care what they thought of me, and by this time I was getting annoyed. I told Francis that he was the head of the project and to 'sort out your side!' — meaning the Tahitian side. Francis is highly respected, because of the Tahiti-nui voyage in 1956, and when he finally said the hull was to remain as planned — end of argument.

So all the canoe builders — these were quite elderly gentlemen, well-respected men — had their noses put out of joint. But as Francis said to them, 'We're not racing to New Zealand — we're sailing, so we're building sailing hulls.'

The worksite Francis chose was at an outer district called Papara, the same district that Francis had left from to sail to Chile on Tahiti-nui in 1956, and it was quite isolated. And beautiful. At my front door was a black sand lagoon, and when it rained the hills behind me came alive with waterfalls. The locals call it 'the land of 100 cascades'. It was absolutely stunning. The people there really adopted me, and they went as far as giving me a Tahitian name — Matahi. I was named after the last warrior the French killed in a rebellion at Ra'iatea in 1893. They gave me his name, and his spirit adopted me. He was a person who refused to be colonised, and I have that concept in me. I don't want to be too influenced by another culture. I'd rather immerse myself in my own culture.

While I was staying at Papara, Gerard and Jeff Sellman made an account for me at the local shop for my weekly food requirements. It was just a small community store, but they were really good to me. The generosity of Gerard and Jeff, especially during the first year when funding was almost non-existent, really stopped the project from falling over. I can't say enough about their contribution or moral support.

Francis chose this particular place because he wanted the worksite to face the western horizon. He wanted to teach me the movement of stars and sun, and the moon and planets in the sky in preparation for the voyage. He himself was living over on the western side of Moorea Island, so that he could familiarise himself with the star patterns moving over the horizon from east to west. So the hull was built facing the western horizon —towards New Zealand.

During the actual construction of the canoe in Tahiti, I sometimes didn't see Francis for months on end. One day I asked him why he was staying away, and he replied that Eric De Bisschop had done that to him while he was building Tahiti-nui, visiting only every few months to check that things were okay. It forced independence on him back then, and that was what he wanted me to get out of it — individual independence; to learn to rely on my own strength rather than look to someone else for strength. Things like that made Francis one of my great mentors.

The building of Hawaiki-nui

Once I had settled in, the first thing I had to do was find the money, the support and some additional labour to help build the canoe shed. That took nearly seven months. All the while the canoes lay in the sand in Papara. I approached the government through OTAC to buy the generator, the timber I needed, and some electrical equipment and tools. They told me that I had to finish the ribs before they would bring in the money and the help. That little task took me six months to complete, adzing all the ribs by hand. I was alone, and didn't have any power equipment at all.

The day I finished my last rib and set it in place, I went straight to OTAC. I was a bit concerned that the government wouldn't keep their side of the bargain. I needn't have worried. OTAC stood by their word and sent a team and the required tools without a fuss. I had to fast-track money from them because I was getting behind, and I needed electric planes to dress the gunnels. Originally I had intended to adze them, but I had run out of time because of the delays. So I translated my knowledge of adze technology to power planes. By early 1983 the fittings started coming together.

First, the gunnels — or freeboards, as they are sometimes called — were lashed to the hulls and ribs. Once they were all in position, we went about attaching the bulkheads. Bulkheads are sort of shaped like an 'O' with a flat top, and are fitted into the hull to support the massive crossbeams that hold the two hulls side by side. Once the bulkheads had been tightly lashed in place, we lined up the two hulls side by side and laid the crossbeams between them. This feature of the construction produced a much stronger crossbeam connection than if we had just lashed them directly onto the gunnels. If we had done that, they would probably have broken off in the first decent choppy sea we encountered.

The next step was to select the trees for the various parts of the canoe we would be working on during the coming months. Francis selected mara for the steering paddles, and we agreed on bamboo for the upper structure and the masts. For the decking and foredeck we chose uru, the wood from the breadfruit tree. Francis had these old canoes that he built some 30 years ago, and this is how strong breadfruit is: they were still intact. I cut them all up, and I used that. It was all uru: beautiful.

A number of graceful old canoes built by Francis Cowan 30 years earlier were cut up for timber after funding had dried up.

The main strength in the construction was the crossbeam fitting that connected the hulls together, and the key to that was the bracing. I didn't have that technology, and once again Francis's experience came to the fore. The secret was the cross-brace between the hulls, and the extra support from the bamboo safety raft that was lashed under the deck between the hulls. The safety raft was a last-minute addition, courtesy of government interference. Despite our resentment at having it forced upon us, its positioning strapped under the deck actually helped stop a fair amount of spray and water from crashing up through the decking and soaking our living quarters.

The other important structures we were working on at that time were the bows. They had to be designed carefully because they would have to meet the power of the ocean full on. I had to think long and hard about how they would be attached to the hull. Francis said all along that it would be best to select a tree for that purpose in Tahiti, and that it should have a fork in it so that it would have a natural curve in the grain. Having a fork would also ensure that it was knotted and cross-grained, so that it would be strong enough to take the pressure from the impact of the waves.

Francis recommended Tahitian timber for the bows, and chose timber from the forks between trunk and branches.

That's the depth of knowledge that Francis brought to the project. I had the technology of totara, but when I arrived in Tahiti I really had to rely on his expertise for selecting the upper structure. He chose uru, which is the equal in quality to totara, and a local imported wood called fallacata. We used an epoxy resin between all of the joinery — for both totara and the Tahitian timber. We wanted to use tapou uru (uru sap) for the caulking, but it took a lot of time to collect and apply it.

Francis's advice was crucial to the whole project. In fact without his knowledge it would have been impossible. I'm more of an artist. I realise now, after all these years, that I'm an artist who likes things to look good, but structurally — I don't worry if it's structurally strong. For Francis, it has to be structurally sound as well as look good.

Francis didn't get his way all of the time, though. He and I would regularly meet to discuss the next stage, and that often ended up in a small confrontation. I always had the upper hand in the end, because he would eventually have to leave and I was left to do the work. More often than not, when he came back the next day I'd have done it my way anyway. Even so, I always listened carefully to his advice.

One example I particularly remember was a three-day argument over the splash-guard — how it was going to look. I told him I wanted a diamond-shaped splash-guard, rather than a single forward-facing V. I was thinking about the backwash. He said it would be all right with just a forward-facing V, but I said, 'In my dream I had a diamond-shaped splash-guard, so I'm putting in a diamond-shaped splash-guard!' He countered,

Francis lashing one hull with nape, or sennit rope. The heavy crossbeams that would hold the two hulls together are resting across the hull.

saying that he was in charge, so I'd better just do what I was told and put in just the forward-facing V. He stayed a little longer than usual to oversee my work, but as soon as he left I went ahead and put on the reverse V anyway. And it stayed there.

And man, in the southern ocean that diamond-shaped splash-guard really helped us. In rough weather the bow would get buried as we crashed down into the next wave. Then as we came up we would have all this water sitting on the hull behind the splash-guard. So when the canoe went back down into the next wave, the weight of the water behind the splash-guard was broken by the reversed V. That way, it didn't carry extra water all the way down when it was buried by the next wave. I always reminded Francis of that: 'See, my dream ...' He'd laugh. 'Yeah, yeah, yeah, well I didn't realise then that you were a dreamer.'

At the same time that we were working on the hulls, we had to start organising things like the nape (the sennit rope made from coconut fibre) for the lashings, and the bamboo for some of the upper structure and masts. Francis managed to contact a man from Raivavae in the Austral Group, who was from a well-known sennit-making family, to start on the sennit. It took them eight months to weave the ropes we needed — about 40 km in all. The bill was huge!

Hawaiki-nui nearing completion at Papara.

The canoe was held together with sennit lashing through something like 3,000 holes, and for every lashing hole we needed a totara plug to seal the gap that remained. Each plug was made by hand. When Francis was lashing, he'd take a plug and personally shape it to fit each individual hole. You can imagine, when you loop through a lashing hole five times, that each hole has a different feature, because the handmade sennit has different widths along its length. It was a very exacting process, and we used no caulking in the holes, just the plugs.

Lashing was another technique that Francis taught me. It's something I'm not willing to share with many people. The tension Francis used was rock solid. On Hawaiki-nui you couldn't so much as move a sennit strand sideways. The secret is in the tension of the sennit when you lever it through the hole, and how you keep that pressure up as the next round goes through the hole. Francis developed a special tapping block shaped to fit in your hand that you use with a heavy hammer, tapping it while the sennit is being pulled by your partner. It really helps to hold the tension. Then you repeat that process, three to five times, depending on where the tension should be in the hull.

As you can probably imagine, we had hundreds of volunteers who wanted to sail on Hawaiki-nui. The way Francis ironed out the selection process was to ask those who were interested to help out with the lashing. That's how we sorted out those who really wanted to be part of the team and those who were only doing the voyage for personal gain.

Because the pressures and responsibilities were going to be so great, Francis would ask anyone who wanted to sail with us to help him lash. After half an hour he would more often than not kick them out because their concentration and discipline wasn't good enough. His argument was that if someone can't put a piece of chicken wire on the end of a lashing rope so that we can thread it through the lashing hole, how's he going to be on the open sea? Francis was going through between three and six people a month. In the end I had to help him, because he couldn't trust their judgement of tension. We went through hundreds of helpers.

One of the major tests during the construction came when we lined up the two hulls side by side and fitted the crossbeams. Until then the hulls had been lying some distance apart, and the ribs had been put in purely by eye. Now they had to be lined up across the two hulls so that the beams would slot perfectly between ribs. There were two pairs of ribs on each hull for every crossbeam: two ribs on one side of the hull, and their opposite. Then you had to match those two with the ribs on the other hull so the beam could slot right across. Just before we began to line the hulls up, Francis said to me, 'Your Maori technology'd better work!' I answered that it hadn't failed yet, but all joking aside it was a huge relief when we lined them up. One or two were slightly out because of the shape of the wood, but we just adjusted the fitting, taking a little bit off the beam, a little bit off the rib, and they slotted in; thirteen beams in all.

The deck covering was probably the hardest part of the final construction. It had to be lashed to the ribs, and they were sticking up from the hulls. I had to try to work out a system to connect the deck to the ribs and hull. Francis had called in to see how things were progressing, and I had to admit I was having trouble conceptualising the whole thing. In the end, Francis had to stay longer than planned to help work out the best way to fit the deck. The ribs that were protruding up from the hulls were acting as mainstays for the bamboo house, as well as being the attachments for the rope stays.

I had to think about what would happen if it rained, or when a wave came onto the deck of the canoe. I really had headaches about how to do the fittings. But we managed it, and it didn't leak when it rained. Using the wood of the breadfruit trees made the job a lot easier because it was fairly water-resistant and it didn't get water-logged. It was a very strong wood.

In my original plan there were two houses on Hawaiki-nui. When it came to their construction, I left the design and choice of building materials up to Francis. He had all sorts of people advising him on the shape and dimensions: 'No, no. The house is wrong! It should be a V-shaped house!' Or, 'It should be a lean-to.' But Francis had his own concept, and it was a half-round house. He designed it to have less wind resistance.

Assembling the different parts of the canoe was exacting work. Here, dowels in the hull are in place ready for fitting the top half of the prow.

The launching of Hawaiki-nui

The day of the launching was 27 November 1984. For some reason Francis had decided to launch the canoe before it was fully completed. I still had a few things to finish, and the cabins weren't yet covered over. The day before the launch, Francis's brother Gerard came to see me. He begged me to try to stop Francis from launching Hawaiki-nui without the official ceremony. It turned out that the government wanted to make a big thing out of the launching, and they were absolutely furious when they heard about Francis's plans to ignore their wishes. I remember Gerard saying at the launching,

'He'll be sorry for this. You don't tell government not to come. They paid for this canoe!'

But Francis didn't care. He just said, 'I want the canoe in the water now.' So he just launched it. About that time the government reduced their support to about 30 percent due to budget cuts. We were supposed to leave in 1984, but that change of heart by the government slowed us down so much that it was another year before we could leave. At the time it was really frustrating, but when I look back the canoe wasn't ready anyway. It took us ten months to perfect the sailing ability of the canoe after the launching.

Hawaiki-nui tied to the wharf at Fa'aa, before the second cabin was removed. The safety rails are also still in place.

Hawaiki-nui was fantastic when she was launched. The whole of Papara, about 1,000 people, turned up for the launching to celebrate and help where necessary. Initially she was hard to get moving, but once she got going she rushed into the water and actually floated higher out of the water than we expected. Of course there were the usual sceptics who were saying, 'It's too heavy. It's going to sink. All those holes in it — the water's going to rush in!' They were betting money on it between themselves. But we had no leaks. Not one bit of water came in at the launch, and I was so elated to see my creation finally floating on the water. It was one of those one-in-a-million moments!

You can probably imagine that by this stage, when the canoe had finally materialised, all sorts of rumours were flying around. It attracted all kinds of cranks. One guy turned up lounging like a mermaid on the hull and my wife asked him, 'What are you doing here?' And he goes, 'Oh, Matahi knows, 'cause he's a god and I'm a god, and we can only communicate as gods.' I didn't even know the guy. I guess it takes all sorts.

The masts were the last of the major components we had to deal with, and they weren't added until after the launching when we had moved to Fa'aa. The masts we chose were bamboo, and we got them from the Musée Gauguin at Papeari. Francis explained that we had to treat the bamboo in salt water for about two to three weeks to cure them. That was so that worms wouldn't eat the bamboo.

The mayor of Fa'aa, Oscar Te Maru, paid for the bamboo. He was also willing to pay for its collection and for people to help us fix the upper deck if we would move our worksite to Fa'aa. It came at a critical time for us. We were getting close to finishing, but we were also desperately short of funds. We really had no option but to leave Papara to take advantage of his offer of help.

Hawaiki-nui was towed from Papara to Fa'aa (we didn't have the masts to sail her) and it was our first opportunity to take her offshore. The guy who was towing us was doing 15 knots constantly and I was steering her with one big steering paddle for three hours — not a problem! People couldn't believe it. Here's this 22-m-long canoe being steered by one person all the way from Papara to Fa'aa into an oncoming sea. I thought we had the perfect canoe. Once at Fa'aa it didn't take long to get the two masts set in place, and we were ready for sea trials.

Well, our first sea trial was a disaster. We tried to sail over to Moorea, where Francis was living. It was only about 22 km from Fa'aa to Moorea, but we had to get towed there. We tried to sail, but it was useless. The original sails we intended to use were hand-woven pandanus ones from Rurutu Island. We trialled them for three days, but they turned out to be too heavy. It took three of us to manoeuvre the sails, which would have been too many in an emergency. So we had to replace them with canvas sails. We did hold on to the pandanus sails, using them for show when we entered or left port.

Soon after our first sea trial, the government approached us because they wanted to display the canoe at the 1984 South Pacific Arts Festival, which had been transferred from New Caledonia to Tahiti after some internal unrest in New Caledonia. They wanted to show off the canoe, and it suited us to get the canoe back to Fa'aa for further adjustments. Once there, we put her up on land to dry.

Until then, I'd never actually seen the canoe on land, as a finished craft. I loved the lines — it appealed to my eye — and it was then I knew the canoe would make it to Aotearoa. It looked right; it just looked like it was the right design.

Over the next few weeks the changes were being made thick and fast. While most of this was going on, Francis was away preparing his mind for the navigating, so he left the alterations up to me. He said to me, 'You know this canoe, you built it — you make the changes from what we've seen in the sea trials.'

Removing the rear cabin and moving the aft mast forward improved the Hawaiki-nui's sailing ability. Here the waka is put through her paces during pre-voyage testing.

So I went to work. I cut the back house off and threw it away. We needed to bring the back mast forward by several feet to improve efficiency, and it would have been impossible to have the second cabin behind the repositioned mast. To conform with safety regulations we had put a rail all the way round the canoe, but it made it look like a stockade so I cut that off. I also reduced the length of the crossbeams because they were a bit too long, jutting out from the hulls. And Oscar Te Maru sent some workers to help Ace and me reset the aft mast properly. We also had to clean the canoe down, repaint it and touch up the anti-fouling, as well as check that all the lashings were still intact.

By then we were ready to recommence the sea trials. Once out of port, Hawaiki-nui showed some of the character that we had witnessed during the first unsuccessful trials. Some days she was easy to turn, and we could normally bring the nose of the canoe around into the wind with a big, long, sculling paddle. But other times she could take as long as two hours to turn. We'd just have to wait and let the canoe get back to her good mood, and then scull her around. I did the sculling because I knew the canoe, I knew her personality. Sometimes I'd even start to talk to her, asking her to co-operate with us.

I think the canoe took on the personality of my great-grandmother, Purewa. She was hard, she was forthright, she believed in the truth and always made people's lives very difficult because of her moral standards. With Purewa being on the left side, the canoe tended to pull to that side.

Her husband, my great-grandfather, was a very big, tall man, and yet this little woman was always ordering him around. And it happened with the canoe, too. She was always pulling the canoe to her side. When we were out sailing and Hawaiki-nui was being particularly difficult, I used to call out, 'Nanny, come on, let me pull the canoe around,' and more often than not she would slowly come around.

In the end it took us about six months to perfect the steering. I had to reshape the steering paddles to suit the canoe's balance. That was our main concern leading up to the voyage. She may look beautiful, but we couldn't control her.

We had all kinds of trials with the steering before we came up with the answer: a permanent centre-board paddle in front of the steering system; that is, one big steering blade. Once again I turned to Francis for his experience. While I worked out how the steering paddle would work — its balance and other technical bits — he worked out the steering-well construction. In the end we managed to come up with the perfect design.

The next hurdle we faced was more red tape. Because the canoe was built in Tahiti, the authorities needed to be sure of its sailing ability before they would let her sail in the open ocean. They sent a civil architect to study the ability of the canoe during our sea trials.

Then the minister of culture insisted we be accompanied by an escort boat during the voyage. This was totally unacceptable to Francis, and it was up to Gerard, as the sort of go-between, to report back Francis's lack of co-operation to the minister. Fortunately, Gerard was able to smooth the waters somewhat, and the minister backed down a little and requested we take a safety raft with us.

The raft the minister supplied was way too big, and would have to have been carried on the deck. This time I refused to accommodate the minister's request. By now Gerard had had enough of running back and forth between the two parties and so we personally purchased a raft that was acceptable to both Francis and me. It was another case of Gerard stepping in to keep things on track.

So we had our canoe and we had our safety raft. The only things that had changed significantly from my dream were the cabin and some of the building materials. I didn't expect a round shape for the cabin. I was going to do a Maori meeting-house shape, that was my original dream. Using bamboo, which is not native to New Zealand, was the other change. It really saved the project because it wasn't too heavy. Bamboo mast, bamboo house and some bamboo decking.

The crew

Francis Cowan was the skipper, and he was by and large responsible for the crew selection. He'd had a lot of experience on the ocean and his strong manner ensured no one forgot he was in charge. Whatever he said, went. The leadership qualities he has can't just be taught. The ability to handle a crisis on the open sea in a canoe held together with sennit rope is something you're born with. He is, in my opinion, one of the great Polynesian navigators of our time.

The crew of Hawaiki-nui. From left to right: Francis Cowan, Greg (Matahi) Brightwell, Rodo Parau, Greig (Ace) Cuthers, Alex Roper.

But before the voyage there weren't many people outside the project team who really believed Francis could captain and navigate Hawaiki-nui all the way to Aotearoa. Those within the crew, however, had absolutely no reason to doubt him. Up until then he had delivered on every promise, every aspect. Take the lashing of the canoe, for example. He didn't go bragging about his ability. He just turned up on the day with his tool box, with all the little gadgets that he made in preparation for lashing, and did his job. And it took seven months! About midway in the lashing all the critics started coming to check if the lashings were genuine. Just by looking at it you could tell he had the expertise. When Francis had to deliver, he delivered. So just on that score alone I had complete faith in his navigational ability.

While I was Francis's right-hand man, Ace was mine. Ace spent almost a year helping me build the canoe at Papara. He was in the story right from the beginning. Ace had been trying to get trees for a canoe in Aotearoa for Francis, while at the same time keeping a lookout for someone who might know how to physically build canoes. I think Ace and Francis had known each other five or six years prior to meeting me. Ace was the self-appointed cook during the voyage.

I'll always remember Ace and his ukulele. In heavy storms I would stay up an extra hour after he took over the shift at 4 a.m. to keep him company. He'd take his ukulele and be steering with his knee while singing lullabies to me and Francis. He was completely at home in the ocean, and his true character came out. Francis always told me, 'Once you're out of the sight of land and you've got nowhere to go, your true character emerges. You either give up or you obey the commands of the captain.' Ace's contribution to the project was without doubt one of the keys to its success. He was outstanding.

Our second navigator for the voyage was Alex Roper. While Francis was skilled as a traditional Polynesian navigator, he insisted we take a second experienced navigator alongside him in case of an emergency, and to cover while he slept. Alex was a Cockney from London with years of sailing and navigational experience behind him. He had known Francis for years, at least since 1956, and had supported him in his dream right through. His main responsibility during the voyage was to work the sails. As sail master, he had to make sure the sails were rigged efficiently for the ever-changing conditions. Whenever one of our ropes got stuck up in the block at the top of the mast, he was the one we sent up to sort it out. He was hauled 12 m up the bamboo mast, in the middle of the ocean, swinging like a pendulum. I don't ever remember him volunteering, but he took it in his stride.

When the crew was announced, the French authorities were a bit put out when an English Cockney was named as second navigator. But it didn't create many problems. His loyalty to Francis was unquestionable.

Rodo Parau from Rurutu was the fifth member of the crew and our fisherman. His fishing expertise and know-how gave us most of our fish cuisine during the voyage. He was a very serious man, and he actually became a crew member on the insistence of the then minister of culture in Tahiti. The minister had insisted a member of his island of Rurutu, the weavers of the sail, be on board with us.

Rodo came on board with experience gained from years of working on inter-island vessels. He was an accomplished coastal fisherman as well. He came to us about two weeks before the voyage and I know he was struggling during the entire three months we were involved in the voyage, whether on land or the sea. He was struggling to cope with the stress and the fear of being in mid-ocean with complete strangers. He didn't know us. He had to become our friend on board Hawaiki-nui. He never hesitated to do anything he was asked, no matter what the sea conditions. I've got only good feelings about Rodo.

So that was our crew. We had originally planned to take a crew of seven, but after the rear cabin was removed we only had room for five.

THE VOYAGE OF HAWAIKI-NUI

Tahiti to Moorea

The first part of the voyage was the short hop from Tahiti to Moorea. Before we left, Francis took me aside for a chat. 'You've done your part. Now I'll show you what my part is all about. And you'll see why the powers that be brought us together, because I couldn't build the canoe without you, and you couldn't sail the canoe without me. And plus, you're married to my daughter, so let's make this voyage a memorable one, and let's do it without any assistance. Let's do it as men committed to a cause.' Our departure date from Tahiti was 28 October 1985.

We had the whole nation watching us leave Tahiti to sail to Moorea —and one of our halyards got stuck in the block. And then the boom twisted so we couldn't pull the main sail up. We sat there for about three hours. In the end Francis rigged up a head sail and we managed to crawl to Paopao Harbour in Moorea. It took us about 8 hours to complete a 40-minute trip. That first leg to Moorea was a complete failure.

It was such a bad start that the government said we would have to prove our sailing ability on the leg between Moorea and Ra'iatea before they would let us leave French territorial waters. It was a real embarrassment and we were very demoralised. The less said about that first leg the better.

When we finally got over our disappointment and were starting to think about the next leg to Ra'iatea, Alex decided to have a cooking box made up with galvanised plates, so we could cook inside the cabin. Before he designed it I told him to measure our cabin's doorway, but he knew better. He said he had it under control. Of course when it came to fitting the cabinet through the door, it was too big.

This cooker business happened during a period of good winds, and I kept telling Francis that we should take advantage of them while the going was good. Francis, on the other hand, saw the value of the box and insisted we delay our sailing to Ra'iatea for two days while I made a new one.

Moorea to Ra'iatea

By the time the cabinet was finally ready, Francis was eager to leave as soon as possible. In the end we stayed at Moorea for three days. A lot of the time was spent preparing ourselves mentally for the challenge ahead. It was something that none of us, apart from Francis, had ever experienced before.

We had another good send-off and crept out of Paopao Harbour about half-past one in the afternoon, and sat in the channel waiting for the wind to come up. We were still there at midnight! I was so depressed that I took Francis aside and told him that if we were still sitting there in the morning I would swim back to shore. He replied calmly that the local wind from the mountains, the hupe (as it is known to the locals), was going to come down and push us out of the shelter of the island between 1 and 2 a.m.

And of course it happened just when he said it would, but the rest of us weren't mentally prepared for it. We'd been sitting around all day doing nothing. The cool winds came down about one in the morning, picked us up and took us out from the shelter of the island. Once out from the island's shelter we hit winds of about 30 knots and took off like a rocket. We were going so fast that we couldn't control that damn canoe — it was too fast. It was so fast that Ace and I were too scared to even stand, and we were reduced to crawling. All the while Francis was laughing his head off and suggesting that we might like to stand up and help with the sailing of the canoe sometime before we got to Ra'iatea.

We didn't really have a roster that first night out of Moorea because we were so excited about finally being under way. We let the canoe run at full speed and didn't worry about the stress and strain on the canoe. We knew she could handle it.

Ace at the helm. As skipper, Francis insisted that the steersman wear a safety harness at all times. Without the harness anyone who fell into the ocean would almost certainly be lost, unless they were lucky enough to grab the trailing rope.

That first show of power by the elements was an opportune time for Francis to remind us of our safety routine. Whenever we were on steering duty, we were to wear our harness at all times. During the sea trials we discovered that by the time the canoe came around to pick up any person unlucky enough to fall off the canoe, it would be too late. It took so long to turn around that there wasn't much chance of a successful rescue. He reminded us to be really focused at all times while on deck.

The only chance we would have if we fell into the ocean without a harness was to grab hold of a rope that we had trailing off the back of the canoe. It was knotted along its length to help anyone grip it if they were fortunate enough to reach it. It was only about 40 m long, so you would have had to have been a quick swimmer to get to it before the canoe dragged it out of reach. The rope had a role in Francis's navigation as well. He kept a regular watch on it to make sure it stayed in a straight line behind us. If the canoe began to veer off course, the rope's angle would change and warn him immediately.

Ace used to make light of the prospect of falling off, to lessen the fear of dying. He used to joke about it, saying things like, 'Well, I won't wear my harness today. I might fall in and wave you guys goodbye on your way to New Zealand!'

We sailed without mishap through until the next evening, when we arrived off Ra'iatea lagoon about 5.30. It was quite rough and just starting to get dark, so we decided to wait outside the reef until the morning. Francis didn't want to risk the canoe, and decided to turn and wait in the Huahine Channel, just off Huahine Island. While we were out there, the waves steadily grew in height. We estimated that at their peak the waves were about 4.5 m high, and Francis made us sit there with no anchor to see how the canoe would ride the waves. As it turned out, Hawaiki-nui rode up the waves smoothly and slid down the other side with the same style. Nevertheless, I stayed with the steering paddle — I wasn't as confident as Francis yet. But the canoe weathered the storm and by morning the winds had died down enough to let us sail into the harbour.

When the authorities saw us sailing into Uturoa Harbour unassisted and under sail they finally believed in our ability. Uturoa Pass is notorious because of the cross-current and cross-break of the tides. The two coral heads are a bit apart — they're not quite in line, one forward and one back, and the waves criss-cross. It's regarded as a very dangerous pass.

We slowed the canoe down, I steered her in nice and gently, eased up alongside the wharf, threw the ropes over, tied it up and prepared for the welcoming ceremony. Hawaiki-nui had arrived safely and without assistance, and we were elated. All those hard years melted away when we sailed into the lagoon using finger-tip steering right up to the wharf and the welcoming party.

Among those in the welcoming group were the president of French Polynesia, Gaston Flosse, and several of his ministers, the mayor of Uturoa, and several other officials from Ra'iatea. There were the usual dances, photo shots and speeches, but to be honest we were more interested in checking the condition of the canoe.

After the ceremony we learnt that we were one of the few vessels that have been able to sail unassisted from the open sea through the lagoon pass into Uturoa Harbour — an early accolade for Hawaiki-nui. The speed of our voyage shocked a lot of people, not least Francis's brother Philip, who had a US$1,000 bet with Francis that the Huahine–Ra'iatea ferry, which left Tahiti the same day we left Moorea, would beat us in to Uturoa. Francis won his bet, and that was our pocket money for the rest of the voyage.

The day after we arrived in Uturoa we sailed around to Mirimiri, the traditional departure point for Rarotonga when sailing from Ra'iatea. We still had plenty to do. We needed to make our final check of the canoe, as well as re-provision our stores. We also had a bit of a problem with the boom, which meant we had to take it off from the main mast, because the tie-down rope wasn't strong enough, and re-lash it.

The officials also insisted that we install a radio for safety before we left French waters. We didn't want to carry a radio at all, because we didn't want people to think we were getting any advice, but the officials got their way in the end.

With all of the work to be done on the boom, as well as the fitting of the radio and re-provisioning, we ended up staying at Mirimiri for five days, departing on 5 November.

Ra'iatea to Rarotonga

After we had said our final farewells to friends and family, Francis gave the order to cast off. One of his friends had agreed to tow us out to the channel where we would raise our sails and be away.

We'd only managed to move a couple of metres when we came to a shuddering halt. We had cast off all right, but had forgotten to haul up one of our anchors that we had put out earlier to stop us from crashing into the wharf in the rising wind. As you can imagine, we felt rather sheepish! Francis grabbed an axe and just cut the rope. Off we went to a rousing cheer, leaving behind one of our precious sea anchors!

Local legend recalls that in times past a fire platform was lit near the shore in the early evening to help with the navigation to Rarotonga. The navigator simply lined the fire up with Temehani, the largest mountain on the island, and kept the two points aligned throughout the night. Then, once the direction had been determined on that first night by the navigator, he could transfer the course to a star path for the remainder of the journey. When we left Ra'iatea we were able to see the fire platform burning right through the night.

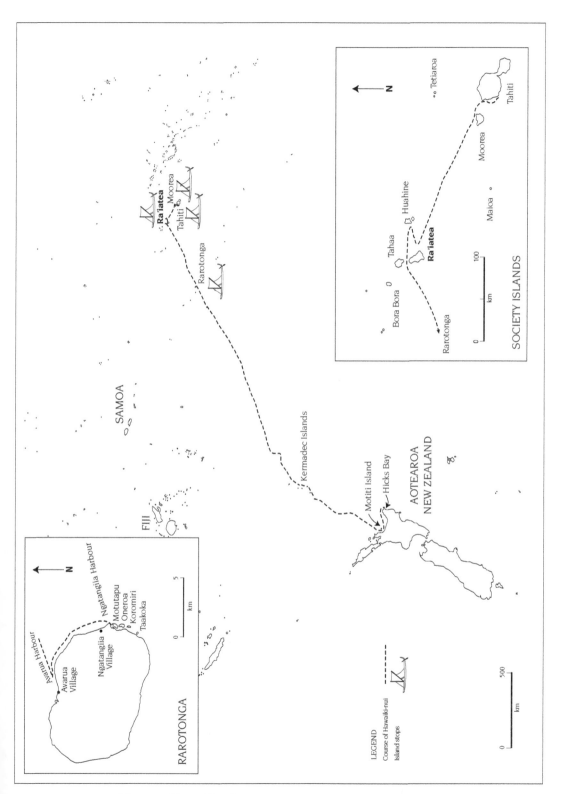

The route of Hawaiki-nui

Once we had set our initial course with the help of the fire platform, Francis was able to show us how to keep on course using techniques he had learned during his years at sea. By observing the action of the streamers we had attached to our sails, he was able to keep us on course. Whenever the wind was blowing constantly from one direction, we were able to use the streamers to detect if we had accidentally changed course. All we had to do was watch the angle of the streamers in the wind — if the angle changed, we were off course.

We also knew that if the streamers began to dip, then the wind was about to change direction. Francis drilled it into us to watch the streamers all the time while on steering duty. He used to say, 'If the wind is going to change direction, the streamers will start to dip up and down as the strength of the wind dies away. Then, when the wind picks up again, you'll know the wind has changed direction because the streamers will be on a new angle.' The streamers were a very important piece of equipment for us during the voyage.

We always got a little nervous when the streamers began to dip, because not only did the canoe slow right down, but there was always the chance that if we had no wind for a long period, we would lose our sense of direction and our course heading. If that happened we would have to wait and realign ourselves during the night with Venus and the Southern Cross.

During the voyage we also used the streamers to forecast winds, which we managed to do with some accuracy. Generally, if the wind was blowing strongly and the streamers were sitting horizontally, we could expect very strong winds for the next couple of days. But when the streamers started to pitch upwards we knew we were in for a hell of a storm. And it didn't take our sail master, Alex, too long to work out that if the streamers started to point stiffly, without fluttering, we needed to reduce the sail area drastically so that we wouldn't be caught unawares by strong winds.

Because the streamers were bleached off-white, they were also easy to read at night, which was essential for safety. It was quite unnerving being caught out by strong winds at night, and it could be potentially disastrous if we got caught by a really strong gale. So the streamers really were vital.

From memory, the wind seldom changed direction during the hours of darkness, but it did seem to increase in velocity, and the swell got decidedly bigger. Even so, the wind was usually pretty consistent from night to night, growing in strength from dusk until about midnight, when it levelled out until dawn, then started to ease off a bit.

One of the more relaxing aspects of the overall voyage was the opportunity to fish. Rodo was our number one fisherman. His ability in tropical waters was certainly unmatched by anyone else in the crew. On the leg to Rarotonga he managed to catch a tuna every second day and a mahimahi every third day. Rodo's big advantage was that he made his own lures during the voyage from the dried skin of fish caught along the way.

After adding tassels to the dried skin and lashing it to a hook, he had a big-fish catcher every time.

As we got closer to Rarotonga we found we had a number of sharks following us. They must have figured that the fish we were catching were an easy source of food. When any of us caught a fish, it developed into a race to get it on board before the sharks got to it. One fish we brought on board already had a huge bite out of it.

On the third day out from Ra'iatea we got caught in a nasty squall, which soon developed into a gale. The seas were monstrous and the winds ferocious. Francis estimated that they got up to about 80 knots at one stage. The winds were so strong that they eventually broke our main mast. In the confusion that followed, Francis's experience and calmness under pressure came to the fore again and saved the day. He knew exactly what to do. He ordered our sea anchor to be put out and had me bring in the steering paddles and rudder to ensure that they didn't get broken or lost in the huge seas. Then he supervised the hauling in of the mast. All the while his calmness helped the rest of us stay composed.

When we were able to have a close look at the damage, we discovered that the front stays that held the mast up had worn and broken under the stress from the storm. It took us 36 hours to set up an effective jury rig and get going again. The repairs reduced the height of the mast considerably, and we were very concerned at that stage that the shortened mast wouldn't allow us to sail fast enough to escape the storm. To our great surprise the canoe seemed to sail as fast as it had before the accident.

My wife had flown on to Rarotonga and was anxiously awaiting our arrival. Of course she was aware of the storm, and was naturally worried for our safety. With the delay caused by the storm damage, we were two days behind schedule. We had originally planned to complete the Ra'iatea–Rarotonga leg in about nine days, but it ended up taking eleven. When we finally made Rarotonga we were still in the tail of the gale. Raipoia was watching us approach the harbour from the beach, and later told us that she was losing sight of the canoe in the stormy seas, so you can imagine how big the sea was running.

When we arrived in Rarotonga, we sailed into the main harbour of Avarua on the northern coast. We came in on the tail of the gale and at night, so it was too dangerous to sail directly to the traditional harbour of Tangiia. In the morning, however, the Rarotongan elders insisted that we be towed around to Tangiia Harbour, down on the south-eastern coast. It was a great honour for us as they allow very few visiting vessels to land in that particular harbour. A few days before we arrived, the Hawaiian vessel Hokule'a had sailed in. She made an impressive sight sitting tied to the wharf at Avarua.

By the time we reached Tangiia Harbour there was a huge crowd to welcome us. In true traditional style we ran Hawaiki-nui up on the beach adjacent to Avana Stream and made an offering to the local elders. We had brought kumara (sweet potato) from Tahiti especially for the occasion, and were delighted when they returned the compliment by offering a Rarotongan variety in return.

Looking back, despite the obvious difficulties experienced in the storm, it was a marvellous leg of the voyage. We managed to catch plenty of fish to supplement our diet, and the canoe performed well in the heavy seas. What

The new mast being manhandled aboard Hawaiki-nui at Avana, Tangiia Harbour. It took the intervention of Sir Tom Davis to secure a replacement mast in Rarotonga.

was especially pleasing for me was that we all felt safe and confident in the canoe's ability.

We were treated very well by the people of Rarotonga. We had feast after feast, and were driven anywhere we wanted to go. People were embracing both us and the canoe. We were being treated so well and having such a good time that we had to be careful not to fritter away our time. We still had to replace our broken forward mast and see to various other bits and pieces that needed attention.

As it turned out, we could only find one suitable bamboo in the whole of Rarotonga, and the owner didn't give a damn about our plight. In the end it took some persuasion from the then Cook Island Prime Minister, Sir Tom Davis, before the woman would part with her bamboo.

In port I always relied on Ace to help me do all the repairs, and we spent nearly two weeks repairing the canoe. Once we finally got hold of the bamboo it took a week of hard work for us to refit the mast. Fortunately, the replacement bamboo had already been cured in salt water, which saved us another two to three weeks, but we still had to construct the new mast. We needed to transfer the crown from the old broken masthead to the new mast, as well as strengthen the mast with a number of bamboo splints. The boom also had to be fitted, and we had to make sure that the lashings for the sails fitted the circumference of the new mast.

The only concern we had with the new mast was that it had a number of very fine cracks all along its length. I had to count them for Francis. He wanted to know how many splits there were that could possibly weaken the mast. I counted 63. I remember because I had to count and mark all of them. After a careful inspection, Francis decided that the bamboo was strong enough. Fortunately for us all, he was right.

We also did plenty of minor repairs: to the supports for the centre-board rudder paddle, some work on the cabin, as well as renewing the ropes for the mainstays on the blocks.

The French authorities at this time decided to upgrade our radio. They actually flew someone over to fit the radio and make sure we knew how to use it. I think they didn't want to be held responsible if anything went wrong.

When we set off from Tahiti I had accidentally left Francis's reading material, about 20 books, in a car during the excitement of the moment, and I can tell you he wasn't too impressed. He thought he'd read all these great novels during the voyage, because when you're sailing well, with no drama or crisis to keep you busy, it's such a boring existence. When we got to Rarotonga all we could scrounge was all these *Watch Tower* magazines from Francis's cousin and a copy of the Koran. It wouldn't be an exaggeration to say that we were almost brainwashed by the time we arrived in Aotearoa! After the voyage Francis commented, 'Well, if we have to describe our routine on board Hawaiki-nui, it was just five bored men, waiting to arrive in New Zealand, 'cause there was nothing to do but read *Watch Tower* and the holy Koran!'

Rarotonga to Aotearoa

A little over two weeks after we sailed into Rarotonga we were ready for the last and longest leg of our voyage. The canoe was ready, and we had more than enough provisions. The people of Rarotonga had come forward and showered us with fresh produce in the days leading up to our departure. The deck was covered with cases and cases of tomatoes, pawpaw, bananas and coconuts. And wild honey. We probably had 20–30 kg of sweet, sweet honey. The honey, along with the fresh lime, was probably our favourite food until it ran out.

As with Tahiti and Ra'iatea, we had a fantastic send-off from the local population. Before we left, the Rarotongans insisted that we erect a stone on their sacred marae site at Ngatangiia. It was to stand alongside the stones for Te Arawa, Takitimu and the five other migration canoes that, according to their traditions, left Tangiia Harbour over a thousand years before us for Aotearoa. It was a huge honour for Hawaiki-nui, and truly an emotional ceremony for us all.

Hawaiki-nui leaving Tangiia Harbour, with the new mast at front.

After the ceremony at the marae, we returned to the canoe for the final speeches and the send-off. We left Tangiia Harbour on 29 November feeling confident, but ran into trouble immediately. I have to take full responsibility. It turned out that the foot of the new mast hadn't been secured to the mast shoe. I don't know how I missed lashing it, but fortunately Francis noticed the mast pitch backwards slightly as soon as we started sailing. So there we were, sitting out in the channel off Rarotonga being jostled around in very bumpy seas while Ace tried to re-lash the foot of the mast with heavy rope. However much we tried, we couldn't correct it, and we certainly weren't in the mood to return to the wharf and own up to it. In the end, Ace managed to do a decent job despite us not being able to risk taking the sail down because we were so close to land, and he secured the mast well enough for us to sail on.

On the 22-day crossing from Rarotonga we had 3 days of fine weather at the most, so we were virtually constantly walking around in wet clothes. Any time it looked like it was going to clear up, out came all the clothes and bedding for airing. The dry spells usually only lasted for an hour or two before it would start to spit again. Then it was a rush to get everything back inside and wrapped up before it got wet. The rain wasn't always a bad thing, especially when we were running short of fresh drinking water. Every time it rained we had a water brigade and caught as much of the water that ran down the sails as possible.

Personal hygiene was something that Francis was particularly hot on. Even so, we could only wash in salt water with a little Lux Liquid thrown in for the suds. We certainly didn't have any flash soap, and, unbelievably, none of us took a mirror along, so our shaving was sort of half-pie as well.

Francis had a big toilet bag with all the goodies inside it that he used to keep in the cabin. Because our lips were cracking and sore, and our skin was peeling off, Ace and I used to get into it while he was asleep during his break from navigating, and put a bit of this mousse stuff on our faces to ease the discomfort. I think Francis knew, but he didn't say anything.

As I said earlier, Ace was the cook for the voyage, as well as being in charge of the rationing. In the mornings we had a light snack to keep us going until the evening, when we had our one main meal of the day, at about six o'clock, which we always ate together. I remember one particular meal early on in the voyage, when we were still well stocked with pawpaw, kumara, coconut, wild honey and dried banana. The menu started off with freshly caught raw fish sprinkled with lime along with a couple of crackers. Then it was the main course of kumara, tropical fruits and honey. Absolutely fantastic! I'd never eaten so well.

It became a daily ritual to ask Ace what was on the menu, and Ace always replied, 'One coconut shared between five of us, dried fruit, and raw fish.' It doesn't sound too appetising, and we only had limited rations, but believe me, Ace put together some memorable meals. The only reason any of us lost weight during the voyage was due to the fear of dying at sea — it certainly wasn't through Ace's cooking.

Each evening after the meal we had to take a look at the food distribution on board. Both the food and water were stored in the two hulls, and if we took too much food or water from one hull it would upset the balance and cause the canoe to pull to the heavy side. We had to redistribute provisions between the hulls on a regular basis to keep a good balance. In the end we only just had enough food for the voyage, because we had been

Ace and Francis enjoying a meal during a quiet spell.

counting on some fresh fish being caught along the way. And, from memory, we were allocated only about 1.5 litres of water each, per day.

As well as being in charge of food stocks, Ace was the second fisherman behind Rodo. Because we were having such a hard time catching fish to supplement our food stores, Ace decided to try to catch a shark. There were a few that were following us, so it didn't take him too long to entice one to take a hook. The only problem was that once we lassoed its tail and got it alongside the canoe, it was too heavy to pull on board. Ace's solution was probably the most astonishing thing I have ever seen. He actually jumped onto the back of the shark — it was still alive — and gutted it right there and then in the water. God knows how many other sharks were nearby! He split its stomach right down the middle and emptied it of all of its guts to make it light enough to manhandle onto the canoe. I really couldn't believe it when he jumped onto that shark. It was incredible.

During the voyage from Rarotonga to Aotearoa, Venus was one of our primary navigation aids. In December Venus was setting on the starboard bow, and could only be seen for three hours each night.

While we were taking our initial direction from Venus, we also had the Southern Cross to our port side. If we went off course it didn't take too long to realise it. Suddenly Venus disappeared from the rigging and the Southern Cross was no longer in place to our left. It was really like we had a narrow corridor to sail down.

We also knew that we were likely to encounter little cloud cover to obstruct our view of the heavens at night during November and December. As it turned out, there were very few nights when we didn't get at least a glimpse of the stars every couple of hours or so, although it was usually clear for most of the night. On the odd occasion when the stars weren't visible for long periods at a time, we were able to use our streamers and the consistency of the wind's direction during the hours of darkness to keep our course. We also had the rope trailer out behind us as an additional aid.

On the last leg to New Zealand, our physical strength was being quickly sapped. Our skin, being constantly wet for so long, started to peel off our faces, fingers and feet. I myself couldn't wear shoes, and was constantly soaked all the way through. During the long, cold, lonely hours through the night I thought a lot about my wife. Before we left she said, 'When you're cold and lonely and afraid, just think of me — my warmth and my support and my love.' Her words helped me a lot.

Along with the physical hardship, we also had to deal with inner fears as well. It's hard to describe, and I don't think you could really capture the feeling unless you experience it for yourself, but the sheer size and power of the sea when you're out there on a small canoe with your life in the hands of the gods can be a terrifying thing. One day I was leaning on the cabin and it was like we were riding on the roof-tops of the waves. I was looking down and could see right to the bottom of these huge troughs. It seemed such a

Alex Roper soaking up some welcome evening sunshine.

long way down, and it was like we were balancing on the edge. I'll never forget that feeling. We tried to put the ocean's power out of our minds, but it was always there, reminding us, haunting us.

Another psychological problem for us came in the shape of the sharks that followed us for well over a week. They were following in our wake, happy to wait for any food scraps that might fall off the canoe or be thrown out after meals. They were big black-tipped sharks, about 4 m long. Francis had encountered them before and described them as the butchers of the sea. They had no fear of anything. After a while they really started to get to us. It got to the point where we had to stop the canoe and let them circle us for a day without feeding them before they would leave us alone.

Going to the toilet was certainly an experience with those sharks hanging around! We ran out of toilet paper half-way through the final leg and had to start sitting off the back of the canoe. Each time a wave came up we'd wash ourselves with one hand, all the while looking out for those black-tipped sharks to come and bite our arses! Our toilet sessions were very fast.

We had previously had an indication of their intent when we caught the shark that Ace jumped on earlier in the voyage. Ace and Rodo cut the head off, took the jaw out, and threw what was left of the head back into the ocean. To our disbelief, its partner actually sat there with its head out of the water, and chewed its mate's head in front of us, all the while seemingly watching us on deck. That sent shivers up our spines. It had absolutely no fear of us whatsoever. It was like he was giving us the message: 'Put your arm, put your hand, put your leg in the water and I'll bite it off. Just try.'

About a week into the Rarotonga–Aotearoa leg, Francis decided that we were being pushed too far to the west, and he ordered the sails to be brought down. We sat there for about four days drifting with the currents. I've got no idea how far we drifted during the four days, but it was hard just sitting there. It transpired that Francis was waiting for a change in the wind direction. The wind was pushing us too far to the west, and Francis had calculated that if we continued on the course we were sailing, we would make landfall up near the Bay of Islands rather than further south as intended. The predominant wind direction was from the south-west, and we just needed it to move a little. Finally after four days it obliged us and we were off again. Not before time either.

It was another three or four days before we came across the Kermadec Chain. From memory, Francis had a booklet that had all the silhouettes of the Kermadec Islands, and he identified the island as L'Esperance Rock. We think it was that, but we can't be sure. Anyway, as we passed the island, Rodo asked Francis to anchor in its shelter so we could swim to the shore with the hope of gathering some birds' eggs. Francis thought about it for a while because he knew we could have done with some fresh eggs, but in the end decided instead to keep going and clear the Kermadecs' notorious waters while the winds were favourable. It was night as we crossed the Kermadec Chain, and Francis took point guard and walked the perimeter of the canoe keeping an eye out for rocks with his big, heavy torch until the crash of the breakers was well and truly out of earshot. I remember it was raining and very cold, and the sea was black and rough. Despite missing out on the eggs, we were very happy to clear the danger.

Another problem we had to worry about by this stage was that both of our steering paddles had been severely weakened. Both paddles had fractures and were flexing quite badly. It was just due to inexperience and the technique some of our crew were using, but it caused a real problem. Rather than letting the canoe run on, they tried to fight the natural run of the canoe and held the steering paddle too rigid. It was a fight the ocean wasn't going to lose.

Despite the hard times, we have a few highlights to look back on as well. Just after the episode with the sharks, Alex showed his experience and played the fool for the good of the crew. One morning when we were all up and about, he jumped out from the cabin, stark naked and wearing an old wig, just playing the clown. His fooling around really came at just the right time for us. It lightened the mood on board and it put the shark fears right to the back of our minds.

A bit later, up by the Kermadecs, we encountered a pod of whales that was probably on its annual migration to feed in Antarctic waters. They never moved any closer than about 200 m from us, but all the same we had no doubts that they were the lords of the ocean. They were completely at home

With the change in temperature from the tropics to southern latitudes, wet weather gear was soon called for.

in their environment. It was an unforgettable experience to be so close to them — just them and us. It was as if we were the only two groups of living things on the planet. An awesome experience.

Another highlight was watching an albatross that latched onto us for the final ten days of the voyage. It was a beautiful bird. I remember it swooping down into the troughs catching fish without even landing, before gracefully flying back up. It was beautiful to watch.

Landfall in Aotearoa

Our official landfall in Aotearoa was Motiti Island in the Bay of Plenty. It took us 22 days to reach there from Rarotonga, and another 10 days to actually land at Hicks Bay on the East Coast. The first clues that we were close to land came about 300 km out from Aotearoa. We were in the open sea and exposed to the elements. Heavy dew in the morning, the insects landing on the canoe and a distinct drop in the temperature were all unmistakable signs that we weren't far from home. Then a couple of nights later we actually saw the long cloud that often sits over New Zealand. We were still about three days out.

After all of our deep-water voyaging, it was the coastal sailing that caused the most problems. We got caught in another storm just off Tauranga and decided the safest option was to shoot out a hundred miles or so and wait offshore for the storm to pass before we made our final approach. It was a hard decision to accept because we were so tired, but we had no real choice. At the same time Francis decided that we should try to contact the emergency channel monitored from Auckland to let them know where we were as a precaution. The radio operator was able to tell us our exact position after we sighted an emergency beacon out at sea and counted how many flashes of the light there were per minute. As it happened we had been pushed further south by the storms and were now off Whangaparaoa Harbour, one of the traditional landing places on the East Coast, just out of Whanau-a-Apanui land. We had to sail offshore again to avoid being wrecked on the coast. It was 28 December, two days before we finally landed.

About this time we were buzzed by an aeroplane just off East Cape. We were running about a week behind schedule due to the storms, and Gerard had flown to Aotearoa and organised a private search. Of course we couldn't have known who was on board the plane, but as it swept down towards us, Francis called out, 'That's my brother. Just like him to do that. To make sure we are safe right to the end.' And sure enough, it was Gerard.

Within a day of being sighted by Gerard's plane, the emergency channel operator contacted the Watties' fishing trawler *Kaiti* and asked her to tow us in. They were concerned because of our ongoing difficulties fighting the storms. That decision left a bit of a sour taste in my mouth, because I believe we could have made landfall under sail with the help of the strong north-easterly that had sprung up. In any case, the *Kaiti* towed us to Hicks Bay, where we landed.

There was a good number of people waiting for us, including my mother and father and brothers. Most of our supporters were still in Auckland, waiting at Orakei marae. Those on land told us later that Hawaiki-nui looked like a ghost canoe as it approached the wharf, with the light shining on the heavy dew. It was New Year's Eve, 1985.

In the morning the locals took everything out to dry in the sun and then cleaned the canoe out. They bailed the water out from the hulls, washed the canoe down and fed us. The last part of the voyage had really taken it out of all of us, but Francis in particular. It was decided that Francis should leave for Auckland as soon as possible because he was very sick.

Even in the comparative safety of Hicks Bay, the tail end of the storm was still strong enough to have one last go at us. With the canoe tied at the wharf, the big swell coming into the bay was lifting her up and banging her into the wharf. I had to make the decision to have the canoe towed around to Whakatane where we would wait for Francis. We would have loved to have sailed there but we were just too tired. We got another great reception at Whakatane, and were happy to rest up for a week before the final tow up to Okahu Bay in Auckland.

When we did get to Okahu Bay we ran the canoe up onto the beach. Although we had been towed to Auckland, and had first made landfall down-country a bit, we got a fantastic reception at Okahu Bay. There were absolutely thousands of people there to see us. Maori and Tahitian representatives performed the welcoming ceremony. It was a special day for all of us who had been involved in the voyage. Francis had recovered enough to rejoin us and led our side of the ceremony.

Life after the voyage

To be honest, straight after the voyage we were too tired to appreciate our achievements. It took me eighteen months to recover physically (I went down to about 75 kg from 88 kg) and at least five years to recover mentally. For a long time I would sleep all day and then wake up in the evening and think that the curtains in the room were sails. I would start to rig them like they were sails.

I found it very hard coming back into civilisation. It was tough to get back into the routine of life on land, and I couldn't even relate to everyday things like hygiene. Communicating with people and accepting people was another problem. The voyage gave me a heightened sensitivity, so that I could actually interpret people's body language, their expression, their vibrations, their thoughts. I soon lost interest in people who for one reason or another weren't genuine.

That attitude used to make people very critical of me, calling me arrogant and stuck up. But it's really not that at all. It's the fact, I think, that the mental stress, the physical stress, spiritual stress and the elements that put all this together make you so fatigued that you just break up. It's like I had a mental breakdown, a physical breakdown. I struggled for five years to get over the experience of Hawaiki-nui. During that time a million things went through my mind. At first I didn't believe we had done it. Then I felt I hadn't done enough, we could have done more. All sorts of strange feelings that I couldn't talk to anyone about.

In the end it took constant nurturing by my wife to get me back on my feet, to turn me back into a human being. Today I'm more of a human being than I've ever been, because I've got over that experience. That's why I'm not too keen to do another voyage for a little while. Because I know the human tragedy it can cause. I caused human tragedy, I stepped on people, I pushed people out of the way, I ignored people — just to fulfil my ambition.

Because the ownership of Hawaiki-nui was formally handed over to the French in Tahiti when we needed financial assistance, the canoe had to be returned to Tahiti after the voyage. Originally it was agreed that Hawaiki-nui would be displayed at OTAC and have a canoe house built for her. I don't know what happened, but the canoe house was never built and the canoe was left to crack and rot in the harsh Tahitian environment.

We tried to negotiate with the Tahitians to buy Hawaiki-nui back for a display at the Maritime Museum in Auckland. Danny Tumahai and I flew to Tahiti on behalf of Ngati Whatua and the Maritime Museum to try to secure her, but we couldn't come to an agreement. Later, after a number of years of neglect, Hawaiki-nui was cut up and the hulls were used for a new canoe, Tahiti-nui. I still find it very painful to talk about it.

AFTERWORD

In 1989, four years after the voyage, Matahi was awarded the prestigious Blue Water Medal by the Royal Akarana Yacht Club. The award was presented by the then governor-general, Sir Paul Reeves, with Francis, Ace and Alex in attendance.

According to the yacht club's rules, the award is given for:

... the most meritorious cruise, either coastwise or deep sea, made by a vessel sailing from or arriving at any New Zealand port, or by any New Zealander sailing between ports outside New Zealand. Provided they consider a nominee worthy of the medal, the judges may award only one such medal in a calendar year.

Matahi Brightwell and his son Tau Puru, with the Blue Water Medal from the Royal Akarana Yacht Club.

The following excerpt acknowledging the award is from the Royal Akarana Yacht Club's 1995 anniversary book.

> 1989 *Greg Matahi Brightwell of the Pahi Tere Hawaiki-nui. Greg hand-built this 21 m twin-hulled canoe in Tahiti using totara logs shipped from New Zealand. With a crew of five, Greg then sailed the vessel from Tahiti to New Zealand.*

The Blue Water Medal is an internationally recognised award and has only been awarded eight times since its inception in 1952.

BIBLIOGRAPHY

Adkin, G.L., *The Great Harbour of Tara*. Whitcombe & Tombs, Wellington, 1959.

Akerblom, K., *Astronomy and Navigation in Polynesia and Micronesia*. Ethnographical Museum, Stockholm, 1968.

Andrews, L., *Hawaiian Dictionary*. Henry M. Whitney, Honolulu, 1865.

Babayan, C. et al., 'Voyage To Aotearoa.' *Journal of the Polynesian Society* 79: 161–200.

Best, E., *Polynesian Voyagers: The Maori as a Deep-sea Navigator, Explorer and Colonizer*. Dominion Museum, Wellington, 1975.
    The Astronomical Knowledge of the Maori. Dominion Museum, Wellington, 1986.

Brower, K., *Micronesia: The Land, the People and the Sea*. Mobil Oil Micronesia, Micronesia, 1981.

Buck, P., *The Coming of the Maori*. Whitcoulls, Wellington, 1987.

Davidson, J., *The Prehistory of New Zealand*. Te Papa Tongarewa, Auckland, 1992.

Davis, T., *Island Boy: An Autobiography*. University of Canterbury Press, Christchurch, 1992.

Dodd, E., *Polynesian Seafaring*. Nautical Publishing, Lymington, 1972.

Elbert, S. and M. Pukui, *Hawaiian–English Dictionary*. University of Hawaii Press, Honolulu, 1957.

Evans, J., *Nga Waka o Nehera: The First Voyaging Canoes*. Reed, Auckland, 1997.

Finney, B.R., *Hokule'a: The Way to Tahiti*. Dodd, Mead and Co, New York, 1979.
    Voyage of Rediscovery. University of California Press, Berkeley, 1994.
    'New Perspectives on Polynesian Voyaging.' In *Polynesian Culture History: Essays in Honor of Kenneth P. Emory*. G.A. Highland et al, eds. Bishop Museum Press, Honolulu, 1967.

Finney, B.R. et al., 'Re-learning a Vanishing Art.' *Journal of the Polynesian Society* 95: 41–90.

Gladwin, T., *East is a Big Bird*. Harvard University Press, Cambridge, 1970.

Golson, J., *Polynesian Navigation. A Symposium on Andrew Sharp's Theory of Accidental Voyages*. The Polynesian Society, Wellington, 1972.

Grimble, A., *Migrations, Myth and Magic From the Gilbert Islands*. Routledge and Kegan Paul Ltd, London, 1972.

Haddon, A.C. and J. Hornell, *Canoes of Oceania*. Bishop Museum Press, Honolulu, 1991.

Hawkesworth, J., *An Account of the Voyages Undertaken by the Order of His Majesty for Making Discoveries in the Southern Hemisphere*, vol 3. Strahan and Cadell, London, 1773.

Holmes, T., *The Hawaiian Canoe*. Editions Limited, Hanalei, 1981.

Irwin, G., *The Prehistoric Exploration and Colonisation of the Pacific*. Cambridge University Press, Cambridge, 1992.

Kane, H.K., *Voyage: The Discovery of Hawaii*. Island Heritage, Honolulu, 1976.

King, M., *Maori: A Photographic and Social History*. Reed, Auckland, 1996.

Kyselka, W., *An Ocean in Mind*. University of Hawaii Press, Honolulu, 1987.

Lewis, D., *Daughters of the Wind*. A.H. & A.W. Reed, London, 1967.

     The Voyaging Stars. Collins, Sydney, 1978.

     We, the Navigators. University of Hawaii Press, Honolulu, 1994.

     'Expanding the Target in Indigenous Navigation'. In *Essays from the Journal of Pacific History*, B. MacDonald, ed. The Journal of Pacific History, Canberra, 1979.

     'Polynesian Navigational Methods'. *Journal of the Polynesian Society* 73: 364–74.

Mildon, K., 'Ocean Cruising.' In *Royal Akarana Yacht Club: Home of Bluewater Sailing*. Ocean Press, Auckland, 1995.

Nelson, A., *Nga Waka Maori*. Macmillan, Auckland, 1991.

Salmond, A., *Two Worlds*. Viking, Auckland, 1991.

Sharp, A., *Ancient Voyagers in the Pacific*. The Polynesian Society, Wellington, 1956.

Siers, J., *Taratai: A Pacific Adventure*. Millwood Press, Wellington, 1977.

Smith, S.P., *The Peopling of the North*. Whitcombe & Tombs, Wellington, 1898.

     'Guiding Stars in Navigation'. *Journal of the Polynesian Society* 27: 226.

Sutton, D., ed., *The Origins of the First New Zealanders*. Auckland University Press, Auckland, 1994.

Thomas, S.D., *The Last Navigator*. Hutchinson, London, 1987.

Trotter, M., and B. McCulloch, *Unearthing New Zealand*. Government Printer, Wellington, 1989.

INDEX